Preaching to the
Black Middle Class

Preaching to the Black Middle Class

Words of Challenge, Words of Hope

Marvin A. McMickle, Ph.D.

JUDSON PRESS
Valley Forge

Preaching to the Black Middle Class: Words of Challenge, Words of Hope
© 2000 by Judson Press, Valley Forge, PA 19482-0851
All rights reserved.

Bible quotations in this volume are from *The Holy Bible*, King James Version (KJV). Other translations are marked as follows: the New King James Version (NKJV), copyright © 1972, 1984 by Thomas Nelson Inc.; the Revised Standard Version of the Bible (RSV), copyright © 1946, 1952, 1971, by the Division of Christian Education of the National Council Churches of Christ in the U.S.A., used by permission; and the New Revised Standard Version of the Bible (NRSV), copyright © 1989 by the Division of Christian Education of the National Council of Churches of Christ in the United States of America, used by permission, all rights reserved.

Library of Congress Cataloging-in-Publication Data

McMickle, Marvin Andrew.
    Preaching to the black middle class : words of challenge, words of hope / Marvin A. McMickle.
        p.   cm.
    ISBN 0-8170-1328-8 (pbk. : alk. paper)
    1. Afro-Americans – Religion. 2. Middle class – United States.
I. Title.
BR563.N4M355 2000
277.3'0829'08996073–dc21   99–37472

Contents

Foreword

ON SEPTEMBER 24, 1895, W. E. B. DU BOIS WROTE A LETTER to Booker T. Washington in which he praised Booker T. Washington's address at the Atlanta Exposition. In the course of the letter, Du Bois wrote, "I congratulate you on having been made by Providence the instrument of such a message...."

One might well, and appropriately, assert that Providence has made Dr. Marvin McMickle the instrument of such a message as is contained in *Preaching to the Black Middle Class: Words of Challenge, Words of Hope.* One says this advisedly, because while many have pondered the estrangement of suburban blacks from inner-city blacks, no one has stated, I believe, the very real problem of such alienation with the thoroughness that Dr. McMickle has brought to this thorny subject. He wisely uses Antioch Baptist Church, Cleveland, historically one of the most creative and influential congregations in America, as an example of a membership in which so many congregants do not live in proximity to the church edifice. This is duplicated times almost without number in black America.

Dr. McMickle's cogent treatment may be considered providential because no issue faces blacks in America with greater potential disaster than this one, threatening as it does the saga of the black diaspora in this land. This internal chasm in black life, with its potential for suspicion and mutual enmity, may compound the evil that the Kerner Commission pointed out in 1968 as two Americas, "one white, one black, separate and unequal."

Dr. McMickle seeks to go beyond diagnosis to suggest ways in which the cleavage between inner-city blacks and middle-class blacks might be lessened.

This eloquent treatise renders us all debtors to Marvin McMickle's trenchant but sympathetic analysis. So seeing this book, we may view it as a gift of God to us all, as we face a new millennium in which, please God, we may close this widening division.

GARDNER C. TAYLOR
Pastor Emeritus
The Concord Baptist Church of Christ
Brooklyn, New York

Acknowledgments

THIS BOOK WOULD NOT HAVE BEEN POSSIBLE WITHOUT the help and opportunities extended to me by the people and congregations with whom I have worked over the last twenty-eight years. I am indebted to Dr. William Augustus Jones Jr. and the Bethany Baptist Church of Brooklyn, New York, where I served from 1970 until 1972. Dr. Jones is my father in the ministry in every way. I was baptized into the Baptist community and licensed to preach by this Prince of Preachers. His early encouragement to pursue every opportunity to write and publish my thoughts has sustained me during the development of this book. I am honored by his recommendation of the book to others.

The late Dr. Samuel DeWitt Proctor afforded me the opportunity to engage in pastoral ministry at the historic Abyssinian Baptist Church of New York City between 1972 and 1976. It was one comment from him in my first year on the staff there that established the basic premise on which this book stands. I regret that he did not live to see this project completed. I regret even more that I never clearly articulated to him how much his mentoring, fathering, and friendship meant to me. Dr. Calvin O. Butts III continues the legacy of pastoral excellence that has been the hallmark of Abyssinian throughout this century, and I am honored to claim him as a friend and brother as well.

The St. Paul Baptist Church of Montclair, New Jersey, was my first pastorate. For ten years, from 1977 until 1986, the congregation there helped me to grow and mature as a pastor. Although I have now been gone from New Jersey for more years than I was present, there are those from that congregation with whom I remain in touch. A choir from St. Paul even traveled to Cleveland, Ohio, at its own expense to participate in my installation at Antioch Baptist Church, where I have served since 1987. The leader of that choir explained, "We did not want to *send* our pastor to you; we wanted to *bring* him here in love." I will always draw strength from that comment.

Needless to say, Antioch Baptist Church of Cleveland, Ohio, has provided me with the inner-city pastoral setting that made possible the analyses found in this book. That congregation has allowed me to engage in civic, political, and academic pursuits and has provided the necessary staff support to sustain the daily operation of the church. All of the sermons found in this book were first preached to that congregation. Their openness and responsiveness to the program suggestions that are outlined in the following pages has been extremely gratifying. If ever a congregation has made their pastor feel welcome to tarry and encouraged to do what has seemed most urgent, Antioch Baptist Church of Cleveland is that place. I love the people there and thank God for bringing us together in the Kingdom's service.

The city of Cleveland has placed me in contact with some of the most remarkable clergy colleagues a person could ever desire. To my friends in United Pastors in Mission, my thanks to each of you for the ways in which you have blessed and encouraged my ministry. I have mentioned you often in this book. To the president and faculty of Ashland Theological Seminary, I also owe a debt of gratitude. Serving on the faculty with you has helped to sustain in me a passion for scholarly pursuits. You help me live out the vision of ministry that Paul defined in Ephesians 4:11 when he said that some are called to be pastors and teachers. I am privileged to do both, thanks to Antioch and Ashland.

I want to thank Randy Frame at Judson Press. He has provided the technical guidance and support that has made this book possible. I deeply appreciate his willingness to work with me until a suitable project for Judson Press could be developed. Whatever good can be said about this book is due largely to his efforts. Of course, whatever flaws may exist in logic or conclusion are entirely my own.

My thanks, too, to Gardner C. Taylor, Jeremiah A. Wright Jr., Otis Moss Jr., and J. Alfred Smith Sr. These distinguished pastors and preachers honored me beyond measure by reviewing the manuscript during its development and then by offering the comments that are printed herein. Each of these men is an accomplished writer and scholar in his own right. That they took the time to consider my work leaves me forever in their debt.

Finally, to my wife, Peggy, and my son, Aaron, I extend my deepest love and gratitude. You make coming home a joy every day. Thanks for allowing me the time away from you that was required for the writing of this book. I hope and pray that both of you will conclude that it was worth the sacrifice.

Introduction

N A 1998 PUBLIC BROADCASTING SYSTEM (PBS) TELEVISION special entitled "The Two Nations of Black America," hosted by Henry Louis Gates Jr. of Harvard University, a question was raised that is the genesis of this book: "How have we reached this point, where we have both the largest black middle class and the largest black underclass in our history?" In both the television special and related Internet materials that followed is a discussion of the social forces that have resulted in this income and class disparity within the black community.

There has long been an awareness that an income gap existed between blacks and whites, as groups, in America. The 1968 Kerner Commission reported that the riots in America's cities in the 1960s erupted as the result of there being two Americas: "Our nation is moving toward two societies, one black, one white, separate and unequal." What was not discussed in 1968 was that the emergence of two black Americas was already under way. This disparity in black America was not based upon skin color, as was so often the case in earlier generations of black America, when light-skinned blacks formed a caste within a caste that constituted a black elite. The division of which I speak, and which the PBS special examined, is based on income disparity. There is a black middle class that is becoming more and more affluent. There is, at the same time, a black underclass that is becoming increasingly impoverished.

The question for this book is what the class disparity within the black community means for the ministry of black churches. More precisely, what are the ministry obligations and opportunities of black middle-class churches that are physically located within America's inner cities? Increasingly, these churches have two separate congregations. One church is the membership that drives into the inner city each Sunday for worship and fellowship. The other church is the people who live in the neighborhood that surrounds the church building, who turn to the church in search of hot meals, Alcoholics Anonymous (AA) support groups, day-care services, and even temporary shelter. In many instances, the first church is composed of people in the middle class, and the second church is composed of people in the underclass. How should the one relate to the other? That is the question this book seeks to address.

I am drawn to this topic because it describes, precisely, the ministry in which I have been engaged in Cleveland, Ohio, since 1987. I see the two nations of black America every day. By and large, the membership of Antioch Baptist Church is middle class. The church has historically attracted persons employed as medical professionals, bankers, financial planners, lawyers, college professors, public-school teachers and administrators, government employees, small-business owners, and entrepreneurs and persons employed in a variety of other fields who earn enough to enjoy a middle-class lifestyle. However, the church is located in the Fairfax section of Cleveland, in which 40 percent of the residents and 60 percent of the school-age children live at or below the poverty level. The ministry challenge that I face is to develop programs and sermons that speak to the needs of the members of Antioch when they drive in from the suburbs or from other areas of the city. That must be done while urging them to fund, or make the church available for, programs that are targeted to meet the urgent needs of those who live within the Fairfax area itself.

This book will focus on how to develop ministries within black middle-class churches that are relevant, first of all, to the actual members of the congregation. Such a book is necessary because up to now those who have written about the black church in America have done so from a "ghetto" perspective. That is to say, they have attempted to address those issues of urgency for those living within the inner city who struggle daily with poverty and powerlessness. That is the focus of the collected sermons of Manuel Scott in his book *From a Black Brother: Sermons from the Ghetto*. That is also the central theme of *God and the Ghetto* by William A. Jones. *Black Preaching* by Henry Mitchell is also written from a ghetto perspective. These are important and insightful contributions to our understanding of how to do ministry in the inner city. Further, issues of injustice, racism, and the encounter between whites and blacks have also been the focus of those who have developed what has been called a "black theology" and a "black hermeneutic." Such texts as *A Black Theology of Liberation* by James Cone, *Black Religion and Black Radicalism* by Gayraud Wilmore, and *Troubling Biblical Waters* by Cain Hope Felder all come to mind. Each of these texts has made a great contribution to our understanding of the way that religion functions within the black community.

Since the civil rights era, class and income disparity within the black community has been increasing, but it has yet to receive a theological analysis. There have been several sociological studies dealing with issues of class in the black community, including *The Black Bourgeoisie* by E. Franklin Frazier, *Dark Ghetto* and *From Plantation to Ghetto* by Kenneth Clark, and *The Black Underclass* by Douglas Glasgow. Indeed, poverty and prosperity present different challenges to human beings. For example, while all black people in America encounter racism, they do not encounter it in the same ways or in the same places. This book focuses primarily on what increasing prosperity is doing to the black middle class and what challenges it poses for black middle-class churches, especially those located in the inner cities of America.

While the black middle class and its churches are the principle target for this book, there is always the question of their relationship and commitment to the black underclass, members of which are in and out of those churches more than the average Sunday-morning worshiper is. Accordingly this book aims to equip black middle-class churches to serve both congregations — the rapidly growing middle class and the rapidly expanding underclass. Each chapter will also offer specific suggestions on sermon themes, or actual sermons, that are relevant for the topics under discussion. Thus, this book is both a study guide on how to do ministry among the black middle class and a collection of homiletical resources for those who preach in that setting.

Chapter 1 will examine the social circumstances that have contributed to the emergence of the rapidly expanding black middle class, noting how the black church has become increasingly populated with people who no longer live in the community in which the church is located. It will also attempt to make the case that class, and not simply race, is a major determinant of the quality of life that black people in America can and will enjoy.

Chapter 2 will focus on the ministry needs of the black middle class, pointing to such areas as encounters with racism despite enhanced income. What are the programs, sermon topics, and support services that are needed to help people who may be under the impression that by reaching a certain economic plateau, they have placed themselves beyond the reach of racial slurs and discriminatory practices?

Chapter 3 is devoted to helping the children of the black middle class remain in touch with the history and culture of their race. Many of them attend schools in which black history and culture are given limited focus. These children were born after the death of Martin Luther King Jr. For them, the civil rights movement is history, and the historic practices that movement sought to eliminate are ancient history. How can the church provide the historical perspective that will give these young people both an awareness and an appreciation for their own history and culture? And how can the church challenge the parents of black middle-class children to incorporate those lessons into the home as well?

Chapter 4 will explore how to challenge the middle-class members of inner-city churches to assume some responsibility for those black men, women, and children who live in the impoverished areas around their churches. Using the biblical motif of Amos 6:1, "Woe to those who are at ease in Zion," (RSV) this chapter will urge black middle-class churches to do all within their power to ease the physical and financial burdens of those who live within the environs of the church. This will involve not only what can happen within the church building or through the use of church financial resources but also how members of the black middle class can function through their work, social, and political circles to affect the policies that perpetuate the conditions that have caused the rapid expansion of the underclass.

Chapter 5 returns to the middle class by focusing on those secular organizations and social activities with which the church must now compete for the time

and money of the black middle class. What should the church say about fraternities, sororities, and groups like Jack and Jill, which often become the network
in which the black middle class operates to the exclusion of the black church?
What happens when the black middle class would rather go to the golf course or
have brunch during the hours when church or church-sponsored programs are
in progress? What should the church say about the television advertisement that
features a black woman saying, "Sunday is for the *New York Times*"?

Chapter 6 deals with the issue of stewardship, specifically how to help black
middle-class Christians be responsible in the handling of their finances, which
includes support for the ministries of their churches at a level commensurate
with their expanding income. If the financial resources of the black middle-class
churches could be marshaled, they could have an enormous impact on black-
owned businesses, on ministries to the black underclass, and on the preservation
of the wealth middle-class blacks are presently accumulating.

Chapter 7 will focus on the danger present in many black middle-class churches
of losing touch with the traditional forms of worship that have been present
within the black church for two hundred years. There is sometimes a tendency
in middle-class churches to turn to European forms of worship, including music
and preaching styles, at the expense of the exuberance and enthusiasm of gospel
music and the Southern roots of black preaching. These are among the ways that
black culture can be preserved and perpetuated from one generation to the next,
and the church can play a crucial role as the curator of a large amount of historic
black culture.

Chapter 8 will acknowledge the fact that not all members of the black middle
class belong to predominantly black churches in inner-city areas. Many are members of black churches in suburban communities or have joined predominantly
white churches. The black middle class assembled in those churches still needs
to be challenged concerning its responsibility to the black underclass, which was
left in the move to the suburbs. And these black middle-class Christians need
to be comforted as they continue to encounter racism in places well beyond the
ghetto. In this chapter, the white pastors of such churches are also part of the focus.
They must be responsible for preaching to, counseling with, and programming
for people in the black middle class who are now members of churches where
black members are a distinct minority.

In 1903, in *The Souls of Black Folk*, W. E. B. Du Bois observed that "the fundamental problem of the twentieth century will be the color line." As we approach
the twenty-first century, class has joined color as the twin problems that now
confront black America. *Preaching to the Black Middle Class* is written as a way
to challenge black middle-class Christians to confront and respond to both of
these issues.

Chapter 1

The Rise of the Black Middle Class

My soul looks back and wonders how we got over.

—*Lyrics to a popular gospel song,*
sung by Mahalia Jackson

I N 1972 DURING MY LAST YEAR IN SEMINARY, I WAS WORKING at Abyssinian Baptist Church in New York City. Despite all of the biblical and theological principles I had garnered from my academic studies, my preparation for ministry would have been incomplete, and any success I have had in ministry would not have occurred, had it not been for the four years I spent at that church. Under the tutelage of Dr. Samuel DeWitt Proctor, I learned principles for the practice of ministry that have served me well in two pastorates, one in New Jersey and another in Ohio, over the last twenty-two years. However, the most important lesson I learned from Dr. Proctor may have come during a casual conversation as we walked from the church to visit several church members who were patients at nearby Harlem Hospital.

As we approached the corner of 138th and Lenox, we saw several black men standing there. The truth is that whenever you passed that corner, you would have seen most of the men in that group standing there. They were always courteous and respectful. They spoke to us as we passed by, and I remember saying to them that day, "How are you brothers doing?" As we continued along Lenox Avenue toward the hospital, which was three blocks away, Dr. Proctor said, "McMickle, except for the color of your skin, you and those 'brothers' don't really have much in common."

I must confess that when I heard those words, I was inclined to object. It was the era of "black is beautiful" and other themes that attempted to build unity among black people. What could possibly be of such significance that it could outweigh the racial ancestry I shared with those men on that corner? This was not the first time that I disagreed with Dr. Proctor. After all, what is it that a young man of twenty-four years of age does not know? But as the years have gone by, I have discovered that he was as accurate in his assessment that day as he was in many other things he so patiently tried to teach me.

The point that Dr. Proctor was attempting to make is that black churches were increasingly becoming middle-class outposts set down in the midst of the blight and poverty of urban America. The people inside and outside the black churches of inner-city America may look like each other, but in terms of values, vocabulary, world-view, and a vision for the future, the socioeconomic factors that divide them are far more significant than the single racial identification that links them together.

The problem that Dr. Proctor was pointing to in 1972 has become even more extreme in 1999. The church was once the center of a community of persons who lived within that immediate neighborhood. It has increasingly become a place where most of the members travel from considerable distances to meet together once a week for a couple of hours and then leave, with little or no contact with the people who actually live in those communities. The car capacity of the parking lots now rivals in importance the seating capacity of the sanctuary because so much of the congregation commutes from locations beyond the community in which the church is located.

The people we lead in worship are not the same as the people we serve in our hunger centers, Headstart programs, and Scout troops. Most inner-city churches serve two rarely interconnecting groups. One comprises congregants who gather once or twice a week for worship and fellowship. The other consists of persons in the immediate vicinity of the church building who are virtual clients. They gather on a daily basis for a hot meal, a meeting of a twelve-step program that aids in the battle against drugs and alcohol, or help in navigating the complexities of some government bureaucracy.

The challenge for inner-city churches is to offer meaningful and supportive ministries, both pastoral and programmatic, to the two groups of people — the middle-class members who commute to the church and the increasingly impoverished people who live in the neighborhood in which the church building is located. Well into the next century, social and economic factors will likely have the effect of creating larger numbers of persons moving into both the middle class and what is being called the "underclass." The fact that middle-class churches will continue to be located in neighborhoods largely populated by people living at or below the poverty level means that these churches will have to find ways to do ministry that is relevant and empowering for both groups.

Black Urban Communities before the 1960s

The division between resident and commuter congregations was not always the case. There was a time when the idea of "the local church" was a powerful force in black America. The church was within walking distance of most of its members. Programs such as Scouting, Vacation Bible School, Halloween parties, camping experiences, and other activities for teens and children were designed largely for the children of families that belonged to the church. Relationships among church members were sustained not only on Sunday morning when they gathered for worship; these people bumped into each other almost daily in the local grocery stores, barbershops and beauty parlors, movie theaters and parks. The church was part of a much larger black community that interacted socially, politically, and spiritually throughout the week.

Economic disparities existed within the community. People who lived in poverty and people who lived in prosperity were both present. However, they were not strangers to one another because people who belonged to the neighborhood church still lived in the community where the church was located. The welfare mother lived across the street from the doctor or dentist. The single mother who worked two jobs to make ends meet knew that her children would pass a federal employee, a small-business owner, or a schoolteacher or administrator as they walked the streets of those neighborhoods. The Greek-letter symbols of black fraternities and sororities were displayed in the windows of every black community in America. You may have been living in poverty yourself, but the promise and possibility of prosperity were always close at hand. And the church was a major part of these communities where black people lived together across lines of income and education.

In the 1950s and early 1960s, I grew up living in the community where our church was located on the South Side of Chicago. The adults I saw in the church were also teachers, librarians, or janitors in the local elementary or high school. The children in the church studied together in the local public library and played sports together in the city parks. The parents of some of my church friends ran a small record store frequented by teens searching for the latest releases from Motown. The president of the usher board would likely be the worshipful master of the local Masonic temple or the worthy matron of an Eastern Star chapter. People in my church did not simply belong to the same political party; they also lived in the same ward and belonged to the same precinct committee. They voted for and complained to the same alderman or city council representative. They planned block-club activities, interfaced with the local police station, and shared in numerous activities at the nearby YMCA. They lived in a black community that was richly diverse in income, education, profession, and aspiration.

It must now be observed that this sense of community was only superficially a matter of choice. The primary reason there was so much vitality in America's inner-city black neighborhoods for so many years, in the North as well as the South, is that racial segregation kept black people in ghettos, defined at first more by race than by income. As described in Lorraine Hansberry's *A Raisin in the Sun*, residential segregation was as common and as intentional in Chicago, Illinois, as it was in Charleston, South Carolina. As a result, people of widely varying professions and income groups lived and worshiped together. Racial segregation was a cruel chapter in American history, and I can remember marching with Martin Luther King Jr. in the summer of 1966 trying to bring it to an end in my hometown of Chicago.

The end of segregation in America's schools, neighborhoods, and public accommodations was a historic achievement, the culmination of hundreds of years of human sacrifice, blood, and tears. However, in many instances the end of residential segregation brought about an unanticipated negative result — the end of closely knit, richly diverse black communities where people of various income and professional groups wept with those who were weeping and rejoiced with those who were rejoicing (see Romans 12:15). As the walls erected by a segregated America were replaced by the doors of opportunity pushed open by the civil rights movement and the progressive legislation of the 1960s and 1970s, these close-knit black communities in the inner cities took on a decidedly different character. Many of the black families who were financially able to do so moved to other neighborhoods in the city or into the long forbidden suburbs that offered them a piece of the American dream. Like the pioneers of the nineteenth century and the immigrants of the twentieth century, these black people ventured forth into sometimes hostile territory. They followed in the footsteps of other ethnic groups in an exodus out of the inner cities. They were looking for better schools, safer streets, or just a single-family home with a front yard and a picket fence.

A phenomenal thing happened with the black middle class after they began their exodus from the neighborhoods of the inner city. They no longer shopped in the stores or played in the parks or even attended the schools in the old neighborhood, but they did keep coming back to their "home church" on Sunday. It may have involved a subway ride in New York, an El ride in Chicago, or a bus or taxi ride from one side of town to the other in other cities across America, but Sunday after Sunday, year after year, they kept coming back to their home church. This was a difference from other ethnic groups. When the various white groups who once lived in the urban areas began their move into the outlying areas of the city and into the suburbs, they built new churches or synagogues in the new communities in which they now lived. Often they would sell their former church buildings to black groups looking to start new churches in the areas that the whites had fled.

To their credit, even after they moved out of the inner city, members of the black middle class would return to their home church every Sunday. However, that sense of home involved the church building itself, not necessarily the neighborhood in which the church was located. With fewer and fewer members of the church still living in the surrounding community, the church was rapidly becoming a place where a transient population gathered to worship and where a resident population turned for social services. More often than not, the two groups did not really know each other, and neither group worked very hard at trying to change that. They shared the same racial ancestry, but beyond that they increasingly had little else in common. This was the point Dr. Proctor was making as far back as 1972.

Black Urban Areas since the End of Segregation

With the end of residential segregation in America, a new type of ghetto was emerging, linking people whose similarities were less a matter of race and far more a matter of class marked by economic disparity. Gone from the inner-city community was the black professional class, the teachers, most of the preachers, and those who worked in corporate America. They were now buying, even building, the home of their dreams. The children of these families were gone from the local public schools. Gone too was the civic and political involvement of these persons, so that the police and other city services did not respond as quickly as they once did. Left behind were people disproportionately defined by poverty, unemployment, a lack of marketable skills, a constant fear of crime driven by the pervasive nature of the illegal drug trade, and a likely history of involvement with the criminal-justice system. Small businesses that once lined the streets of inner-city America were gone; their display windows were either boarded up or smashed in because the clientele that these stores once served was gone.

In "Integration's Casualties," Russ Rymer contends that the only freedom that integration brought was the freedom to consume such things as housing, education, and especially certain retail and consumer items once purchased from black-owned businesses. It did not allow black-owned businesses to freely operate in the larger economic world of white commerce. Thus, blacks were free to shop and spend outside of their once-closed communities, but at the expense of "the stores and banks — insurance companies and beach resorts — to which they had long been relegated." Rymer says:

> Integration became the greatest opening of a domestic market in American history, but the windfall went in only one direction, with predictable, if unforeseen, results: the whole economic skeleton of the black community, so painfully erected in the face of exclusion and injustice, collapsed as that exclusion was rescinded. In this way, integration wiped out or humbled an important echelon of the black community — the nonclergy leadership class that had fought so hard for civil rights and was needed to show the way to pragmatic prosperity.

Whether they had moved away to live in another area or had gone out of business because of the loss of their customers and clientele, the loss of this black professional class from among other members of the black community was, as Rymer suggests, "an unintended side effect of integration itself."[1]

But at least once a week, the parking lots of the local churches would be jammed with the cars of those who were driving into the inner city to worship in their home church. In the church I now serve in Cleveland, the people inside the church are largely middle-class people. Many of them own their own businesses or hold executive positions in major corporations or managerial positions within governmental agencies. There are a good many medical professionals, college professors, public-school teachers and administrators, real-estate agents, and supervisors and foremen in industrial and manufacturing firms. They live relatively comfortable lives in more than twenty towns scattered over three counties in Greater Cleveland.

Meanwhile, the surrounding neighborhood reflects upward of 40 percent unemployment, with the number of school-age children living in poverty being above 60 percent, according to the 1990 census. Those numbers will likely show an increase following the census in the year 2000. Crime is an increasingly serious problem, and 80 percent of all crime in Cleveland is related to the use, sale, or possession of illegal drugs. The people inside and outside the church may be similar in skin color and racial background, but their daily lives are similar in few, if any, other ways. What is true for us in Cleveland is equally true for many black middle-class congregations across the country, and this presents significant challenges for those of us committed to doing ministry in America's inner cities.

This is the lesson that Dr. Proctor was trying to teach me in 1972. Long before sociologists began talking about the relative impact of race versus class within the black community, Samuel Proctor was already telling me that class was as important a factor as race, so far as life within America's inner cities was concerned. Over the intervening years, I have come to understand that ministry in the black community has to be done by people who clearly understand that preaching sermons and offering solutions to community problems that are solely race based will not be an adequate response.

Certainly those race-based answers to social ills will continue to be useful as black people speak to the larger society about the continuing legacy of racism in America. We must continue to challenge white society to end the racist practices that date back to colonial America. Only then can reconciliation between the races be achieved. However, even when racism is the issue that needs to be addressed, it must be understood that not all black people experience racism in the same ways. Sometimes racism is as blatant as a police sweep gathering up whoever happens to be on any given corner in urban America. Racism can be as crass and blatant as being called a "nigger" by someone who is openly advocating a philosophy of white supremacy. Other times, however, racism takes the form of white realtors who refuse to show homes in certain suburban communities to black families who have the money to buy but whose presence is still not wanted. With increasing frequency, racism takes the form of black contractors who can get business only from public-sector agencies because white-owned private businesses are still refusing to do business with black-owned firms. Racism today reflects the absence of black people from upper management and from the corporate boardrooms of America. The ministry of the black church, while situated in places where racism is most often blatant and apparent, must also be helpful to people in the middle class and the upper middle class. They experience a form of racism that may be subtler but is just as offensive and painful.

However, while race-based discussions may need to go on between the races and at every level of government, serious discussions and an increasing awareness about class distinctions within the black community must also occur. Many voices within black America are attempting to alert us to the fact that class is as significant a problem as race. While *race* may define the discussion between black and white people, it is *class* that will increasingly define the conversation among groups of people within black America. This is the point that William Julius Wilson is attempting to make in his classic study *The Declining Significance of Race*. In that 1988 book, Wilson states, "Race relations in America have undergone fundamental changes in recent years, so much so that now the life chances of individual blacks have more to do with their economic class position than with their day-to-day encounters with whites."[2]

It is time for all easy pretenses of homogeneity to be set aside. Calling one another "brother" and "sister" does not constitute authentic community. And balling up our fist and shouting slogans about racial solidarity at whatever television camera might record our protests may not accomplish as much as we would like to think. If black middle-class churches located in inner-city areas are to have a meaningful ministry directed both toward their own spiritual needs and toward the people who live in those communities, then this class division must be recognized.

Two Nations Separate and Unequal

In 1968, the Kerner Commission investigated the reasons for the riots that had set cities ablaze in racial violence over a series of long, hot summers. Beginning with the Watts section of Los Angeles in 1965, riots spread to Detroit, Cleveland, Newark, and many other cities as well. The commission concluded that the riots were the result of a staggering economic disparity with which black Americans were no longer willing to live. The now famous words of the Kerner Commission described that economic disparity this way: "Our nation is moving toward two societies, one black, one white—separate and unequal."[3] What that commission did not report is that even then black America was becoming two nations, separate and unequal. James Baldwin wrote about this issue in 1955. In *Notes on a Native Son*, he said:

> Aunt Jemima and Uncle Tom are dead, their places taken by a group of amazingly well-adjusted young men and women, almost as dark, but ferociously literate, well-dressed and scrubbed, who are never laughed at, who are not likely ever to set foot in a cotton or tobacco field, or in any but the most modern kitchen.... Yet, there are others who remain, in our old idiom, underprivileged.[4]

Cornel West in *Race Matters* points out that there has always been a black middle class in America, whether defined by complexion or economic status. The difference today is how large that group has become. He writes:

> Black America has had a variety of different middle classes — Free Negroes in the pre–Civil War period; educators, artisans and shop-keepers during the Reconstruction period; business persons and black college professors in the years of Jim Crow laws; and prominent athletes, entertainers and white-collar personnel after World War II.[5]

However, West points out that until the civil rights period of the 1960s this group of middle-class blacks never constituted more than 5 percent of the total black population. Today, the black middle class has jumped to well over 25 percent of the black population in America.[6]

C. Eric Lincoln, in a 1975 essay entitled "The Middle Class Mentality," states that prior to the civil rights era, the basis of class distinctions within black America was largely an internal caste system. All black people in America were the victims of white racism. However, within the black community was a "caste-within-a-caste." It represented an attempt of light-skinned blacks to impose upon their darker fellows new caste conditions quite as inflexible as those with which they were already burdened.[7]

The Urban Institute reports that looking at the growth of the black middle class does not tell the whole story about how class divisions within black America are occurring. One must also look at what could rightly be called a "black upper class," consisting of people who earn upward of $75,000 annually. People who earn between $25,000 and $75,000 annually now account for nearly 50 percent of black America. However, nearly 3 million black people live in chronic poverty with incomes at or below $13,000 for a family of four.[8] These people live within the shadow of the steeples of the great black congregations of urban America. And as Dr. Proctor observed in 1972, the two groups have very little in common beyond the color of their skin.

Harvard Sitkoff also points out how the income gap that now divides black America has grown tremendously over the last thirty years. Writing in *The Struggle for Black Equality*, he states:

The majority of whites in 1992 lived in the suburbs, while an even larger majority of African Americans lived in the inner cities of the nation's largest metropolitan areas.... And within the increasingly black cities are unequal African American societies. In 1990 dollars, 30% of black families earned more than $35,000 annually, compared to 23.8% in 1970. Approximately another third of the black population is lower middle class, earning between $13,000 and $35,000. A third of African Americans, and half of all black children, live below the poverty level defined in 1990 as $12,675 for an urban family of four, and $9,736 for a family of three.[9]

This is an economic picture of what Sitkoff calls "unequal African American societies." There is also an emerging profile of social conditions that helps define these class distinctions. In the PBS special "The Two Nations of Black America," five characteristics emerged that define the group of people who remain confined in the inner cities of America: (1) single female head of household, (2) welfare dependent, (3) marginally educated (high school or less), (4) chronically unemployed, and (5) criminal recidivism (in and out of jail). By comparison, escape from captivity to poverty, and/or closing the gap between the two "unequal societies," involves avoiding the majority of these five conditions.[10]

The Rise of a Large Black Middle Class

The expansion of the black middle class would have been unimaginable had it not been for laws such as the 1964 Civil Rights Act that opened doors of economic opportunity long closed to black people. Bart Landry in his book *The New Black Middle Class* notes that prior to 1960 the black middle class was limited to such professions as "teacher, minister, doctor, dentist, lawyer and social worker."[11] By the mid-1970s, Landry reports that middle-class black people worked in no less than sixty-five different job areas, including accountant, engineer, sales manager, policeman, scientist, and architect.[12] In making this observation, Landry follows by thirty years comments made by E. Franklin Frazier in his two landmark studies of the black middle class— *The Negro in the United States* and *The Black Bourgeoisie*.[13]

Landry reminds the reader that the original group of black professionals that constituted the black middle class were people who "provided services to the rejected."[14] By that, he meant that in a segregated society black professionals served a captive clientele that was prohibited from receiving the same services from white providers. The original black middle class emerged as that group of people who provided the medical, legal, educational, culinary, landscaping, hair care, funeral, and other basic consumer services of a black community whose business was either not wanted by or was not accessible to white society. It was a twofold restriction in that black professionals were limited to a certain number of career paths, and black consumers were limited to those blacks who provided needed services.

As segregation was first lessened, and then eliminated, there was a positive and a negative effect. The negative effect was that the original group of black professionals had to share their once captive clientele with the far larger pool of white service providers. Many blacks were not able to remain in business because their customers left them to do business in the larger white society. The positive effect was best described by Frazier: "The most important consequence of the increasing occupational differentiation of the Negro population has been the emergence of a sizeable black middle class."[15]

The jobs and professions to which black people could now gain access allowed them to engage in what Henry Louis Gates calls "the narrative of ascent." He says, "Blacks are wedded to narratives of ascent, to borrow a phrase from literary critic Robert Stepto, and we have made the compound preposition 'up from' our own: up from slavery, up from Piedmont, up from the Bronx, always up."[16] It was now possible for one generation of black people to attend schools, enter professions, buy homes, and enjoy a quality of life inaccessible, and largely unfamiliar, to any generation of blacks that had preceded them.

Gates offers the following statistical perspective that helps to chart the rise of the black middle class. He reports that in 1950 only 5 percent of black workers held managerial or professional jobs; in 1998 the number was over 20 percent. The number of black families earning more than $50,000 has quadrupled since 1967 and doubled in the '80s alone. In 1973 the top one hundred black-owned businesses had sales of $473 million; today the figure is $11.7 billion. In 1970 only one in ten blacks had attended college; today one in three has.[17] While things have changed for the old black middle class, things have greatly improved for the new black middle class.

The positive and negative effects upon the black middle class that followed the end of segregation can be illustrated by reference to my wife, who grew up in a small town in northeast Georgia during the days of racial segregation. As a result of those policies, she went to an all-black school for her elementary and secondary years. In the mid-1970s the school system finally decided to comply with the *Brown v. Board of Education of Topeka* ruling of the U.S. Supreme Court, issued in 1954, that called for an end to segregation in public education "with all deliberate speed." This is a town that drained the city-owned and -operated swimming pool rather than integrate it and allow black and white children to swim together. This is a town that closed the only movie theater within thirty miles rather than allow blacks to sit anywhere but in the "blacks only" balcony.

Rather than acknowledge that they were ending a segregated system, the school system called for "consolidation," which carried the sense of being a good business decision with a cost-saving rationale. However, when consolidation took place, it was the black administrators, teachers, and other personnel from the formerly all-black schools who were dismissed. On the other hand, today that same small town in Georgia has black police officers, and now the principal of the predominantly white middle school is also black. As controversial as it has proven to be, the intervention of the federal government has been decisive in opening doors of opportunity that have allowed the black middle class to grow in two distinct ways. First, the black middle class has grown as a result of the number of jobs now available to black people that were closed to them only one generation ago. Second, the black middle class has grown as more black families live within the range of $25,000 to $50,000 in annual income.

Poverty versus Prosperity within the Black Community

The painful fact about the emergence of this greatly enlarged black middle class is that the poverty of many in the black community has risen as fast as the prosperity of others. This raises difficult questions about how to do ministry. What are the spiritual needs of the middle-class people inside those churches? What has upward mobility and migration out of the inner city created for them in terms of stress, new forms of racism, and new associations and organizational ties that rival the church for people's time and financial support? At the same time, what are the outreach responsibilities of those black middle-class churches to the people in the surrounding neighborhood who very likely relate to that church more as clients than as congregants? What can and should be the interplay between the transient and the resident members of the community where these churches are located?

The future of ministry for black middle-class churches located in inner-city areas is mirrored in an essay by Clarence Page of the *Chicago Tribune* in his book *Showing My Color: Impolite Essays on Race and Identity*. He writes passionately about the conflict his wife experienced as she made the move from growing up in a public-housing project on Chicago's South Side to becoming the first black woman columnist and first editorial board member at the *Chicago Tribune*. She wrote an essay for *Newsweek* entitled "The Black Middle Class Burden." In that essay she says, "I am a member of the black middle class who has had it with being patted on the head by white hands and slapped in the face by black hands for my success."[18]

Even when black people do arrive into the relative comfort and security of the middle class, no one but themselves seems happy that they have arrived. Their white peers think that it was only because of affirmative action. The blacks they grew up with in the "projects" now view them as Uncle Toms and sellouts to white society. These situations present serious ministry challenges for congregations that must reach in to the wounded blacks sitting in its pews and reach out to the wounded souls standing on the nearby corners. Henry Louis Gates says that more and more black people are "succeeding more and enjoying it less."[19] This is because on the one hand, they are keenly aware of the racial gap that divides them from their white colleagues on the job and in a multitude of social settings.

On the other hand, they are equally aware of the growing economic disparity that separates them from other black people. This is what Samuel Proctor was trying to tell me in 1972.

These are the challenges that await those who will do ministry among the black middle class as we move into the twenty-first century. Writing in 1903, W. E. B. Du Bois stated that "the central problem of the twentieth century would be the problem of the color line."[20] It must be acknowledged that as this century comes to an end, color is not the only problem that confronts us. There are unique pressures being felt by black people in America largely as a result of economic disparity. These class-based questions cannot be dismissed as if race is still the only thing that matters.

Clarence Page refers to some in the black community as "racial romantics." These are people, he contends, "who would have us believe that class essentially does not exist in the black community. Anyone who believes otherwise is quickly and resoundingly denounced and dismissed as some sort of a bourgeois conceit."[21] Page is correct when he observes that "a new black middle class has grown up since the 1960s. It has its own neighborhoods, organizations, magazines (*Essence, Emerge, Image,* etc.), social circles, and grievances."[22] There have always been class differences within black America, but the number of black people who had broken into the middle class had remained modest until recently. Thus, for the vast majority of black people in America, race and color were the defining issues as they sought to find their place in society. That simply is no longer the case for a large portion of black America.

The Weakening Power of Race in Daily Life

Racism has certainly not gone away. The brutal death and dismemberment of a man in Jasper, Texas, who was dragged several miles along a dirt road while tied to the back of a truck clearly remind us that racism is alive and well in America. So, too, do the chance encounters with racism that all black people in America experience, no matter at what level in society they operate. But it cannot be denied that things have drastically changed in this country over the last thirty years. In his book *The Origins of the Civil Rights Movement,* Aldon Morris describes what life was like for black people, especially in the South, prior to the 1960s. He speaks of a "tripartite system of domination in which blacks were controlled economically, politically and personally."[23]

The economic domination involved limiting blacks to the most menial jobs that paid the lowest wage. He reports that in the South in the 1950s, 75 percent of black males worked in unskilled jobs. The political domination involved a dual effort to keep blacks from becoming voters and, as a result of that, preventing any black person from ever holding any meaningful political office. Most especially this meant that such political positions as the county sheriff and the entire criminal-justice apparatus were controlled by whites, who used those of-fices to control blacks. Any attempt to break out of the position of powerlessness was met with brutal force, either by law-enforcement officials like "Bull" Connor in Birmingham or Jim Clark in Selma or by local thugs like the Ku Klux Klan or White Citizens' Council. Following a bombing, beating, or lynching, black vic-tims of that force, guilty of attempting to exercise their constitutional rights, had no place to turn for relief or redress of grievances.

The personal domination involved segregation itself and the emotional and psychological effects of being daily reminded of one's second-class status. I can re-member as a four-year-old child taking a train ride from Chicago to Washington, D.C., to visit my family there. When the train arrived in Cincinnati, all the black passengers had to leave their seats throughout the coaches of that train and move to the car behind the coal car because the next stop for that train would be in Kentucky, where segregated seating was the law. This combination of economic deprivation, political powerlessness, and daily personal humiliation was the face of racism that most black Americans knew before the enormous changes brought on by the civil rights movement. Racism is still with us, but like a once powerful hurricane that has lost most of its force to terrify and to destroy, racism has lost its power to define the terms and limit the sphere in which the majority of black people must live.

Race versus Class in the Post–Civil Rights Era

It is impossible to understand what is occurring within black America without recognizing the issue of class as well as race. This will be especially true for the children of those who lived through the civil rights era. Young black people, like my own son, Aaron, born after the death of Martin Luther King Jr., are becoming increasingly disinterested in the attempts by their parents and teachers to define everything in life in strict racial terms. They actually have no frame of reference that allows them to see the world through that lens.

Nothing better illustrates this point than the sons of two famous black lead-ers of the civil rights and protest era: Jesse Jackson Jr. and Harold Ford Jr. Jesse Jackson is, of course, the noted civil rights leader and former presidential con-tender. Elected in 1974, Harold Ford was the first black member of Congress from Tennessee. Both fathers have long been identified with a political agenda that favored the use of the federal government to protect the constitutional rights of black people. Both sons see class and economics, not race, as the issues that most concern them. Both of them serve in the U.S. Congress. In 1999, Jackson was age thirty-three, and Ford was twenty-nine. In a full-page story in the *New York Times* in March 1998, Jackson Jr. comments that "the color that matters most is green.... Ninety percent of the racial debate is about economics."[24] In a feature story in the *New York Times Magazine* in October 1998, it was noted that Ford Jr. shuns racial politics and votes for such economically conservative programs as a capital gains tax and school vouchers and against such social issues as a needle exchange program for addicts. In that same article, Albert Wynn, a black congressman from suburban Maryland, helped to explain the economic conservatism of Ford Jr. and other young black members of the House: "It's a realistic assessment of where politics is going: toward a middle class orientation as opposed to an exclusively poverty-oriented approach."[25]

While these two young congressmen are working inside the Capitol, a similar shift in political focus is going on within the municipal government of Washington, D.C., as well. Longtime mayor Marion Barry, who was a master of racial politics dating back to his days as a founding member of the Student Nonviolent Coordinating Committee (SNCC) in 1960, did not seek reelection. He was replaced in January 1999 by Anthony Williams, a forty-seven-year-old certified public accountant who is more interested in economic development and racial coalitions than in the confrontational politics of his predecessor.[26] Williams is not alone as a youthful mayor who prefers economic issues over racial politics. Other black mayors such as Michael White in Cleveland and Kurt Schmoke in Baltimore also fit that profile.

Also relevant to the focus of this book is the discussion about Harold Ford Jr.'s home church in Memphis:

> Thirty-one years ago, there were only three other college graduates in the church besides the pastor; now half the adults have earned degrees. Comfortable neighborhoods have replaced public housing. Mount Moriah-East is wealthy enough now to offer college scholarships. Harold Sr. talked to the father who was the janitor at the bank. Harold Jr. talks to the son, who is a vice president of the bank.[27]

The challenges presented by race and class must be addressed within the black community, and especially within and among black churches. This must take place in inner-city churches where the encounter between black poverty and black prosperity is repeated every week. It also needs to take place in the black and white suburban churches where many in the black middle class have gone, perhaps to escape the sights, sounds, and smells of poverty. It must take place among older black people who continue to interpret their existence in America through the lens of race. And it must take place among younger black people who, in their eagerness to move beyond the history of black suffering and oppression in America, may also be leaving behind much of the historic culture of black America that is well worth preserving.

In Matthew 25, Jesus tells the parable of the great judgment and provides the criteria upon which some will inherit eternal life with God and others will be condemned to hell and eternal damnation: "Inasmuch as ye have done it unto one of the least of these my brethren, ye have done it unto me" (v. 40, KJV). For most of my life, I have heard that parable told as a way of challenging white society to respond to the needs of the long-oppressed black masses. Today I hear that parable in a new way. I now understand that it also applies with equal force to those of us in the rapidly expanding black middle class, who have little in common, except the color of our skin, with those blacks living in poverty right outside the doors of the church where we worship. We are the ones who have to guard against ignoring or blaming those who are imprisoned, impoverished, or chronically infirm. It is the job of those who preach and teach among the black middle class, in white churches as well as in black churches, to be sure that both the comfort and the challenge of Matthew 25 are clearly communicated.

I must preach to my mother's generation, defined by the Great Depression of the 1930s and a lifetime of exposure to the ugliest forms of racism. I must preach to my own generation, learning how to navigate the waters of political and economic opportunity that we marched and picketed and prayed to win for ourselves when we were teens. I must also preach to my son's generation, for whom interracial dating, a personal computer, a room of one's own in a privately owned home, and disposable income is all they have ever known. If the church is to have a relevant ministry as it moves into the twenty-first century, we must begin speaking less about race and more about class. The words of William Julius Wilson must be carefully considered: "…the life chances of individual blacks have more to do with their economic class position than with their day-to-day encounters with whites."[28] I first began to understand this when I casually inquired, "How are you brothers doing?" to a group of black men standing on the corner of Lenox Avenue and 138th Street in New York City in 1972.

Dr. Proctor was correct when he observed that except for the color of my skin, I did not have much in common with those men standing on the corner of 138th and Lenox. It began with the fact that I was employed and they were not. I had finished college and was one year away from a graduate degree from a premier theological institution. Many of them had already dropped out of high school and possessed no marketable skills. I happened to be at that corner because I was on my way to a work-related assignment. By contrast, that corner was their destination.

Dr. Proctor did not mean to suggest anything about the human worth and value of the thousands of black men and women who stand on hundreds of corners in dozens of cities across America. In raising the issue in this book, I do not mean to disassociate their presence on those street corners in urban America from national economic policies that are clearly racist either in intent or effect. Instead, I mean to suggest that as far as the ministry of the black church in urban America is concerned, we must operate with a dual focus.

First, we must argue for and work for those remedies that already exist that can improve the quality of life for those who are presently standing on the corners of urban America. There are ways to move people off of corners and into jobs, training centers, chemical-dependency workshops, and homeless shelters and back into school with provisions for child care and flexible schedules. There are proven programs that help ex-convicts reenter society and avoid returning to the custody of the criminal-justice system. All of this can be done, and churches must lead the way in challenging society to move in this direction. We must constantly challenge American society to "let justice roll down like waters and righteousness like a mighty stream" (Amos 5:24, rsv).

On the other hand, black churches in inner-city neighborhoods cannot act as though all that is required of them is that they ball up their fist at the first available white person and cry racism. While issues of race are being worked out, the black churches of urban America must reach out and respond to the human and emotional needs of those persons on the corners of our cities who have no place else to turn but toward us. And the point that must be made is that the only thing we may have in common with them may be the fact of skin color. They may or may not belong to our congregations. They may or may not share our core value system. They may or may not even appreciate the efforts that we make on their behalf. But ministry in urban America now demands that black churches provide as much as possible in the way of direct social services as well as guide persons in the community to locations beyond the church where other services can be found.

Chapter 2

Confronting Modern Racism

Comfort ye, comfort ye my people.
—*Isaiah 40:1, KJV*

I N THE BOOK OF JONAH WE ENCOUNTER A PROPHET WHO attempts to flee from God rather than be faithful to the preaching mission he has just been assigned. In the words of the TV series and full-length film *Mission Impossible*, Jonah was choosing not to accept his mission. Why does Jonah go to Joppa and catch a ship bound for Tarshish to the west when his mission was to travel to the city of Nineveh far to the east? The answer to that question is of far more importance than whether or not Jonah was actually swallowed by a great fish.

The story of Jonah is one of the earliest and clearest demonstrations of intentional racism in the Bible. Jonah did not want to go Nineveh, even though it was a great city with a rich culture, because Jonah did not want to share with the people of Nineveh the benefits of being children of God. The book of Jonah provides no other basis for Jonah's refusal to preach the message of salvation to the Ninevites. No reference is made in the book to any historical conflicts between Israel and Assyria. Jonah himself mentions no personal experiences that he had had with anyone from Nineveh that serves as the basis for his refusal to deliver to them the message of glad tidings. Yet Jonah does not want God to save "them." Jonah does not like "those people." God calls Nineveh "a great city" and wants to see the people of the city brought into the light, but Jonah does not want to share his status as a member of the chosen people with "those people."

In Luke 4, two stories stand side by side, and it is surprising to discover which one generates the most negative reaction among the Jewish people to whom Jesus is speaking in his home synagogue in Nazareth. In verses 18–19, Jesus quotes from Isaiah 61 and declares himself to be the long-awaited Messiah of Israel. Having heard what might have been considered a blasphemous statement, that the messianic promise was being fulfilled in the man who sat before them, the people simply say, "Is not this Joseph's son?" In verses 25–26, Jesus says that in the days of Elijah the love of God was extended to a widow woman from Sidon and in the days of Elisha the love of God was extended to a leper from Syria. According to verses 28–29, when the people in the synagogue heard this, everyone was filled with rage and attempted to throw Jesus headlong off the edge of a cliff.

Why would the claim by Jesus that he was the Messiah be met with such apparent calm by the people of Nazareth, while the claim that the love of God could be extended to Phoenicians and Syrians be met with such hostility? It seems that whatever the status of Phoenicians and Syrians might be in the eyes of God, the Jews in Nazareth were not prepared to embrace "those people" as their brothers and sisters, any more than was Jonah. The "chosen people" were not prepared to open their circle and acknowledge that any other group but theirs was entitled to the benefits that come with being God's elect. Jesus claiming to be the Messiah in the presence of those who had watched him grow up is one thing. Daring to insinuate that God could love a widow in Phoenicia or a leper in Syria as much as God loves any Jew nearly cost Jesus his life.

The Forms and Effects of Racism

These two Bible stories, one from the Old Testament and one from the New Testament, serve as a good point of departure for discussing how racism follows the black middle class no matter how far from the inner city they as individuals move and no matter how much they may accomplish in their chosen fields of endeavor. There remain in America some white people who still do not want to share what Derrick Bell calls "the value" that comes from simply being white in America.[1] Black people, no matter their income, educational attainments, or professional status, still encounter white people who, on a daily basis, attempt to withhold from them some of the benefits and advantages that come as a result of nothing more than being born white.

Such racism, with accompanying pain and anguish, is a reality that the black middle class cannot escape no matter where they live. They still encounter white people in America who do not want "them" in their neighborhoods, their schools, their workplaces, their social circles, and their private clubs. It does not matter if "those people" hold Ph.D. or M.D. degrees, maintain their lawns as well as anyone else on the block, or conduct themselves completely in accord with all the rules of social etiquette and public decorum. There are many whites in America who, in the spirit of Jonah and the people of Nazareth in Luke 4, simply do not want and will not welcome "those people" into their community.

Ministry to the black middle class, while it must challenge them to be mindful of and responsive to the needs of blacks in the underclass who remain in the inner cities, cannot stop there. It cannot be assumed that racism is reserved for those who live in poverty, whether in the physical confines of urban ghettos or the equally impoverished rural areas throughout the American South. Those who minister to the black middle class must also be sensitive and responsive to the pains that racism still inflicts upon upwardly mobile black people who may have been deceived into thinking that their economic and employment status had finally placed them beyond the reach of racist words and deeds.

In a 1985 article in the *Journal of Preaching* and in an unpublished doctor of ministry project for Princeton Theological Seminary, I discuss at length the issue of how the black middle class continues to encounter racism in American society. In the article, the following point is made:

> Our relative economic security does not exempt us from the realities of racism. Black people living in the most affluent regions of the suburbs are still treated contemptuously by their white neighbors. The forms of discrimination may be more conspicuous in the inner city regions than they are in suburban areas. But the intent remains the same: to assign black people to a "place" within society beyond which they are not permitted to go without white approval.[2]

Such a lesson was learned some years ago by several black members of the United States Secret Service, men whose job it was to protect the president of the United States and other high-ranking government officials. A white waitress in a Denny's restaurant in suburban Maryland refused to serve these men solely because of her prejudices concerning black people. What a contradiction this is for our society. Here are men competent enough to be entrusted with the life of the most powerful man in the world, and at the end of the day, they can be denied service in a restaurant by any white waitress who decides that she does not want to serve black people. People in the black middle class face this incongruity in American life every day.

The pain of racism at this level is that it does not come solely from those who occupy positions of power over those in the black middle class. It comes when a white cab driver will not stop to pick up a black man, who may earn in one month what the cab driver may earn in one year. It comes when a black person enrolled in Harvard or employed by IBM is asked by a white person either to hang up a coat or park a car simply because that black person is standing at the door of a restaurant. Who the black person is personally or professionally seems of little or no interest to most white people. It is the fact of being black that determines how black men and women will be met and measured in many areas of this society.

Racism Involving Members of Antioch

Within a one-month period of time, several families in my congregation shared with me the ways that racism has continued to follow them into what they thought were the most unlikely places. One man who is a certified public accountant and a business entrepreneur enrolled his son in one of the most exclusive private schools in the Greater Cleveland area. He called me to report, in the most passionate way imaginable, his outrage over the use in an English class of a book that contained several short stories that regularly referred to black people as "niggers." This was not *Huckleberry Finn*, whose use of this racial epithet has long been discussed. More importantly, this was not a history class, where the uses of that term could be placed within some historical context. Instead, this was an English literature class in which the white teacher saw absolutely nothing problematic about assigning readings to that disproportionately white group of students that referred to black people as "niggers."

When the matter was brought to the teacher's attention, there seemed to be very little interest in the problem that this terminology posed for the student or for his family, who was paying several thousand dollars per semester to enroll him in that school. When the matter was taken up with the headmaster of the school, after such a meeting was reluctantly granted, the response was not much more sympathetic. Other black parents acknowledged that they had suffered similar indignities while having their children enrolled in that school; however, it was something they had decided to endure in exchange for the advantage that such an education provided for their children.

During the same month, one of our congregational members called me from a state university here in Ohio to report that the black student cultural center on that campus had been vandalized by white students. Phrases such as "niggers go home" were painted on the walls of the center. As a sign that racism has high-tech practitioners, e-mail messages bearing hateful, racial slurs were also sent to the computers in the center and to many black students on campus. It took several days for the university administration to address these issues. Finally, the students had to disrupt traffic on the campus in order to get anyone to pay attention to their concerns about racism on that elite college campus.

Finally, the mother of a young woman who attends our church periodically told me about the experience of her child at a private college in western Pennsylvania. This young woman was assigned a white roommate who, according to the mother, "had trouble dealing with diversity." Nothing the black student did was right as far as the white student was concerned. No attempt to be friendly or even cordial was received by the white student. Finally, one day while the black student was in class, the white roommate moved out of the room without warning or farewell and moved in with another white female student. Having grown up in Shaker Heights, Ohio, which is famous for being an integrated community, and in a thoroughly integrated school system, this young black woman encountered such blatant racial prejudice with shock and disillusionment.

Chapter Two

Other Examples of Racism

Two things must be said about the experiences of Antioch's members. First, these are not isolated incidents. Such things happen to black people every day, and not just in ghettos but on the campuses of elite colleges and prep schools. It also happens in the corporate headquarters of companies like Texaco, where white executives were heard on tape referring to black employees as "the black jelly beans in the bag that no one wants to eat."

Second, these forms of racism are far more subtle and sophisticated than those faced by black people as recently as fifty years ago. Black people are now free to vote but are seldom, if ever, endorsed by either major political party for any statewide or national offices. Black people can now manage, perhaps even buy, stores and businesses in which their grandparents might once have been refused service, but they discover that despite a prime location not much white business walks in the door. Black people are now free to move into any home for which they are financially able to secure a mortgage but still may not be welcome in the neighborhood. My wife and I moved into a home in Montclair, New Jersey, in 1977; however, it was over two years before any of our neighbors even spoke to us. Today we live in Shaker Heights, Ohio, and we still have neighbors who live on an adjoining property who wish that we were not here.

Black people can now constitute the entire starting team in football or basketball on campuses where their parents could not be enrolled as students just thirty years ago. But competent and qualified blacks are still not being hired by college or professional teams for responsible positions, whether on the sidelines or in the front office. When they are hired and do not succeed, their failure is frequently attributed to assumptions about race. Such was the case with Al Campanis, former general manager of the Los Angeles Dodgers, who observed that "blacks do not have the necessary tools" for leadership.[3] Yet, when a white coach fails, not only is he or she frequently hired again by another team, but also the failure is never associated with race or ethnicity.

White people in America tend to be evaluated on individual merit. Black people are still subject to being evaluated on the basis of color. While this is a problem for all black people, it is a particular dilemma for the black middle class, for those who are upwardly mobile. They have risen up in society. They have followed the rules that were said to lead to success. They have secured a quality education. They have worked hard on the job and positioned themselves for advancement through the corporate ranks. But at some point along the way, their personal qualifications are overshadowed by their group affiliation. To refer to the words of Martin Luther King Jr. in his famous "I Have a Dream" speech of 1963, people in the black middle class soon discover that they are still judged by the color of their skin, not by the content of their character.

Modern Racism

People tend not to value these concerns about racism because forms of modern racism are not as dramatic as a lynch mob hanging a body from a tree or a hooded Klansman brandishing a rifle at any black person daring to test the laws of segregation in the Deep South. But make no mistake about it, the effect of all forms of racism is profound. In all instances, a benefit of citizenship, a constitutionally protected privilege, or a basic human right is being denied solely on the basis of race.

In a series of workshops on diversity training, Valerie Batts, then of the University of North Carolina, shared with a group of Greater Cleveland business and civic leaders her concept of "modern racism." She acknowledges that for most black people in America racism is no longer practiced or expressed as it was prior to the 1960s. Today, racism offers a softer face, but the result is still "targeting a group within society for less of its society's benefits." She defines racism as "the power individuals and groups of one race use to systematically oppress those of another race. The power bases through which this oppression takes place are government, big business, education, and other institutions such as the church and the judicial system."[4] These are precisely the areas of employment and civic activity where the black middle class is moving in the greatest numbers. The closer they get to the centers of influence in these institutions, the greater the oppression they will face.

In her description of modern racism, Batts addresses four ever-widening areas of influence. First, there is *personal prejudice*, which is the collection of values, attitudes, and behaviors, often acquired involuntarily, that leads one to believe in the inferiority of persons from other racial or ethnic groups. Second, there is *interpersonal racism*, in which any given white person may not hold any personal prejudices against blacks but will withdraw from a conversation or cordial relationship with a black person if another white person views them together and seems to disapprove. In short, some whites may prefer to maintain good relations with whites who hold to racial prejudice rather than risk those relationships in favor of expressing their own open acceptance of people regardless of race or ethnicity. In the words of Dr. King, "America will not only have to atone for the hate-filled words of the bad people. It will have to explain the appalling silence of the good people."[5]

Batts moves on to *cultural racism*, which is the institutional expression of the superiority of one race's cultural heritage and values over that of another. In this expression of racism, certain forms of music or food or certain types of hairstyles may be discouraged as being "too black" or "inappropriate for the office." It was surely cultural racism that was being exhibited in 1997 when golfer Fuzzy Zoeller urged Tiger Woods not to order fried chicken, spare ribs, or collard greens for the meal Woods was planning for the winners of several of golf's major tournaments. It is also cultural racism that has led so many black people to use skin-lightening products like Nadinola and to have their naturally curly hair straightened and dyed so that they look more like white people. With cultural racism, beauty is not in the eye of the beholder; beauty is defined by the white power elite.

I vividly remember traveling through Senegal, West Africa, in 1992. In that former French colonial nation, Africans with extremely dark skin are the largest consumers of these skin-bleaching and -lightening products. Thirty-five years after the French granted independence to Senegal, cultural racism is still at work. One hundred and thirty-five years after the Emancipation Proclamation, many black people in America still feel the pressure to prefer William Shakespeare over August Wilson, Wolfgang Amadeus Mozart's compositions over the Negro spirituals, and Handel's *Messiah* over Mahalia Jackson's rendition of "My Soul Looks Back and Wonders How I Got Over." Cultural racism is with us to this day.

Fourth, Batts mentions *institutional racism*, which typically involves what has come to be known as "the glass ceiling" in the institutions of power. No written laws exist to enforce this practice. And no vote of any group was ever recorded to cement any agreement or understanding. It just becomes apparent that there is a level beyond which few, if any, black people are able to move. This form of racism involves such measurable issues as tenure on university faculties, partner status at various professional firms, senior-executive status in corporate America, or election to boards of directors and trustees for the institutional power bases in local communities across the country or at the national level.

Institutional racism affects blacks in three distinct ways:

> Black people working as professionals in a predominantly white environment live under a daily pressure to prove to their white colleagues, and often to themselves, that they deserve to be where they are. . . . Black people still remain locked out of many areas of corporate, academic and political life. . . . Even when they are admitted to the upper echelons of those fields, they still face continued exclusion from that social network of private parties in private clubs where so many professional relationships are fostered, and where so much important information is shared.[6]

With institutional racism, some blacks are allowed into the inner circle of power, but not many. At the level of corporate directors, it tends to be the same black people, like Vernon Jordan, who are selected. And they are the ones perceived as least likely to disturb the status quo. It is this practice that caused Randall Robinson to speak so harshly about Vernon Jordan in his book *Defending the Spirit*. Robinson says, "Some blacks in Privilege have a loss of memory of what they came to Privilege to accomplish, and further, any memory of the millions camped outside the gate."[7]

The Role of the Preacher

What principles can be set forward that can serve to inform those whose ministry involves large numbers of persons in the black middle class? First and foremost is an awareness of where members of the congregation live and work and an awareness of the ways in which they may be encountering racism so that the pastor can speak to that aspect of their experience. Sometimes these issues will be brought to the pastor/preacher's attention by the members themselves.

The pastor can also learn much about the things that are affecting the black middle class through involvement with groups such as the NAACP or Urban League or by attendance at meetings of the local school board and city council. A careful reading of some of the magazines that are targeted to the black middle class will also provide insight into some of the issues of concern within that group. That would include such periodicals as *Ebony, Jet, Black Enterprise, Essence,* and *Crisis.* The assumption here is that quality ministry does not occur when the pastor stays in the church office, sitting behind the desk, waiting for the phone to ring. In the words of Isaiah 40:11, the pastor should "feed the flock like a shepherd," knowing the needs that must be met throughout the congregation.

The Preacher as Priest

Those who serve among the black middle class must appreciate the role of the pastor as priest as defined by Peter Paris in *Black Religious Leaders.* In that book, Paris argues that there have been four historic roles out of which black preachers have operated over the last two hundred years: the *priestly, prophetic, political,* and *nationalistic.*[8] There may be times when the preacher to the black middle class will operate out of each of those roles, but the role of the preacher as a priestly figure cannot be overlooked.

In *The Souls of Black Folk,* W. E. B. Du Bois observes that the priestly role has been the dominant form of ministry employed by the black preacher dating back to the antebellum era of American slavery:

> He early appeared on the plantation and found his function as the healer of the sick, the interpreter of the Unknown, the comforter of the sorrowing, the supernatural avenger of wrong, and the one who rudely but picturesquely expressed the longing, disappointment, and resentments of a stolen and oppressed people.

Du Bois continues to explain the evolution of the plantation preacher into the black preachers of today by saying, "Thus as bard, physician, judge, and priest, within the narrow limits allowed by the slave system rose the Negro preacher, and under him the first Afro-American institution, the Negro church."[9] There are times when the black preacher must operate out of the other models of ministry, whether interfacing with his or her own congregation or with the wider society, but when it comes to helping the black middle class cope with and respond to the realities of racism, the priestly role is a useful model of ministry to employ.

Paris describes his understanding of the priestly role by saying, "Priests have helped the people to endure those things they could not readily change and to make constructive use of every possible opportunity for self-development under the conditions of bondage."[10] This idea that a priestly ministry is designed to help black people cope with those things they cannot change is supported by Edward Wimberly in his book *Pastoral Care in the Black Church*. Wimberly reminds the reader of the four classical forms of pastoral care in the history of the Christian church: *healing, guiding, sustaining,* and *reconciling*. These four forms of pastoral care are well examined in *Pastoral Care in Historical Perspective* by Charles Jaekle and William Clebsch.[11] Wimberly argues that when it comes to racism's effects upon blacks in America, only the ministries of guiding and sustaining are effective. Healing and reconciling are not possible, says Wimberly, because only whites in America can bring about the end of racism in America and the physical, economic, and psychological wounds it inflicts:

> Guiding and sustaining have been dominant functions in the history of pastoral care in the black church.... Reconciliation took a secondary position, and healing became very difficult because of the racial climate.... The racial climate in America, from slavery to the present, has made sustaining and guiding more prominent than healing and reconciling. Racism and oppression have produced wounds in the black community that can be healed only to the extent that healing takes place in the structure of the total society.[12]

The focus on the need for a priestly approach to ministry is discussed by J. Deotis Roberts in *Roots of a Black Future: Family and Church*. Roberts identifies the priestly and the prophetic as the two traditional forms of ministry in the black church: "The priestly ministry of black churches refers to their healing, comforting, and succoring work. The prophetic ministry involves its social justice and socially transforming aspects."[13] In speaking about the importance of a priestly approach to ministry, Roberts says:

> A people who know the meaning of suffering from long experience with it need a faith that brings comfort and assurance. The tears of Jeremiah, the anguish of Habakkuk, and the patience of Job have tested and challenged our faith through the long night of oppression. The Judeo-Christian faith, filtered through the suffering of blacks, has developed into a tower of strength for survival and meaning.[14]

Roberts acknowledges that all people experience some form of suffering. He says, "All humans suffer because life has its moments of pain and disruption, physical, psychological or spiritual."[15] That is true for black and white people and for people in every income and professional group. However, says Roberts,

Victims of structural oppression bear a double portion of suffering.... Much of their anguish is caused by pain inflicted upon them (individually or as a group) by other human beings. Oppressed people need an adequate faith to sustain them as they face the reality of their lives as persons, families and as a people.[16]

People who do ministry among the black middle class must be prepared to engage in this priestly function to help guide and sustain a group that must cope with the racial climate in America that they are not able to resolve on their own.

The Place of Preaching in a Priestly Ministry

In an oft-quoted observation, C. Eric Lincoln says, "The black church has traditionally relied upon a preached theology."[17] He made this comment in an article in *Christianity and Crisis* in which he was calling for more of the theology of the black church to be written and codified, as has been the case among white theologians for centuries. However, almost thirty years after his comment, I believe it is safe to say that most black preachers still use "a preached theology." Thus, those who do ministry among the black middle class must make good use of their preaching opportunities.

Using a preached theology is not unique to the black preacher. No less a figure in the history of preaching than Harry Emerson Fosdick was the premier practitioner of preaching as counseling. The preaching style of Fosdick is examined in a full chapter in a biography by Robert Moats Miller entitled *Harry Emerson Fosdick: Preacher, Pastor, Prophet*.[18] Fosdick's method of preaching as counseling is also analyzed in a study by Edmund Holt Linn entitled *Preaching as Counseling: The Unique Method of Harry Emerson Fosdick*.[19]

Donald Capps, in *Pastoral Counseling and Preaching: A Quest for an Integrated Ministry*, also discusses the importance of viewing preaching as a time and place for dealing with many of the problems that confront people every day. Capps states:

> When preachers enter the pulpit they become counselors. They may proclaim the gospel, exhort parishioners to lead more godly lives, instruct them in the fundamentals of the Christian faith, and speak out against social injustice. But their main purpose is to give parishioners wise counsel for dealing with life's problems.[20]

"A preached theology" is one effective way to help the black middle-class Christian cope with the realities of racism.

Putting Racism in Perspective for the Minister

It cannot be overstated that issues of racism and other forms of social injustice are not the only themes that must be addressed by those who do ministry among the black middle class. As Roberts reminds us, "Life has its moments of pain."[21] Thus, whoever ministers among the black middle class must be informed, first and foremost, by the category of ministry mentioned by Paul in Ephesians 4:11, "And he gave some to be…pastors and teachers" (RSV). Death and sickness will continue to intrude, and a sermon on racism will not bring comfort. Instead, loving pastoral care and the ministry of presence must be exercised. Drugs and alcohol will continue to create casualties, both physically and emotionally, among the black middle class. HIV/AIDS is no respecter of class and income divisions. Pastors must be aggressive in teaching about, and planning programs that discuss, these behavioral and lifestyle issues. As Paul says in Acts 20:27, the pastor must continue to "preach the whole counsel of God" (RSV). We must continue to examine the great doctrines and disciplines of the Christian faith in our preaching and teaching ministry.

The church should equip people to faithfully confront whatever comes in life, from divorce to disease and from teen pregnancy to terminal illness. However, as Roberts reminds us, "Victims of structural oppression bear a double portion of suffering."[22] Everybody has to deal with "life's moments," but in America, black people and other minorities must also deal with structural oppression, with what Valerie Batts calls "modern racism." People in the black middle class encounter racism in ways that are often unique to their economic, educational, and employment status. They often find themselves in places where the black underclass would never be present. The assumption might be, therefore, that the middle-class black person has "arrived" at a place where they are beyond the reach of racism. They quickly learn that there is no such place in America. It is with an awareness of this reality that ministry to the black middle class must be undertaken. One need not dwell on it every day, in every sermon, at every Bible class, or at the outset of every counseling session, but it cannot be ignored. It is one of the major frustrations in life for the black middle class.

Preaching out of Personal Experience

As a basis for dealing with racism in preaching, I am informed by another insight from Capps. He says that the preacher needs to possess some authority to speak on the issue that has come as a result of his or her own experience with the issue:

> The pastor needs to acquire and maintain a clear position on the problem preached about. Such conviction is acquired through personal experience and direct observations. His own life, the behavior of his immediate family, observation of the contemporary scene, the knowledge of human nature gained by personal counseling, and witnessing the power of God at work in the transformation of individuals all contribute to giving form to the preacher's conviction.[23]

This is good counsel because each of these areas allows the pastor to learn firsthand how racism continues to impact the lives of people in his or her congregation, in the larger community, and in American society. As a result, the pastor is preaching with the authority that only personal experience with the problem can provide. The preacher does not have to say, "This is what happened to me." But the preacher can say with confidence, "I know that this is what is happening," which is a particularly important point for white pastors who have members of the black middle class within their congregations. They may not have had any personal experience being the target of racism, but it is possible for them to hear from and learn from those who have had such encounters.

Moving beyond Issues of Racism

It is important that a ministry geared to the black middle class not dwell on the issue of race but return the congregation to areas where it can respond to the suffering and oppression of others. Black people are not the only people to suffer from discrimination. Having several persons of Native American heritage in my own congregation has sensitized me to the fact that their suffering in this country began sooner, has lasted longer, and has not been addressed in ways that equate with what the federal government has done for African Americans. Part of the challenge for ministers in black middle-class churches is to move people from self-pity and the perpetual preoccupation with black victimization and to focus on the suffering that other groups have endured and continue to face.

For the last twelve years, Antioch Baptist Church has shared in an interfaith relationship with a Jewish synagogue in the Greater Cleveland area. Over the years, our reflections about the Middle Passage and the auction blocks of slavery have been tempered by their firsthand experiences with Auschwitz, Mauthausen, and the other Nazi concentration camps during the Holocaust. Together we viewed such films as *Schindler's List* and *Amistad*, followed by a discussion that involved youth and adults. In that context, we have been able to gain a better understanding of how racism has affected other groups around the world. Compared to the sufferings that we heard about in these sessions, the racism that we have personally experienced seems less significant.

A Trip That Changed My Life Forever

In 1995 I was invited by the owner of the company that does the heating and cooling work for our church, a Jewish émigré from Hungary, to return with him to Austria for the fiftieth anniversary of his liberation from Ebensee, a labor camp for Jews and other nationalities from all over Europe during World War II. He had been taken prisoner in 1944 at the age of fifteen, weighing 155 pounds. He was liberated in May of 1945, weighing less than ninety pounds.

We visited several of the camps to which prisoners were shuttled as the Germans tried to hide the horrors of the camps. I stood next to the crematorium. I saw the openings in the walls where prisoners could be shot in the back of the head during interrogation or torture. I looked down on the camp in Melk from a Roman

Catholic monastery, where the priests who lived there during those years could not help but see the smoke rising from the ovens that burned the bodies of those who had died from starvation, disease, or sheer brutality.

I saw the pain and anguish etched on the faces of the former prisoners who were reliving what they had heard, seen, and felt upon their own bodies on that very ground fifty years ago. After having visited those camps, I have never been able to speak about racism in America without remembering that the suffering of black people in America is not the only example of humanity's inhumanity worth my consideration. Every black person of whatever income or class group needs to be reminded of the experiences of Native American throughout the Western Hemisphere and the European Jews during the Holocaust. From a contemporary perspective, the evidences of black-on-black ethnic cleansing in Rwanda and Burundi and white-on-white ethnic cleansing in Bosnia and Albania are an important reminder that the misery one human being can impose upon another is not always a matter between different racial groups. More importantly, these instances of ethnic cleansing and outright genocide are a stark reminder that not many black people alive today have suffered to the same degree as have those whose plight we see every night on the evening news.

All that being said, in light of white racism and structural oppression, the need clearly does still exist within the black middle class to be encouraged, to be guided and sustained.[24] That work is best done by persons who operate out of a priestly model of ministry. In so doing, we bring to life the words that Jesus read in his home synagogue as described in Luke 4: "to heal the brokenhearted" (v. 18). We are also able to equip people with the spiritual resources that allow them to sing the words of the gospel song, paraphrasing a verse from Job, that says "Lord, help me to hold out until my change comes."

Going beyond Our Comfort Zone
Acts 1:6–8

I MAGINE THAT YOU ARE SITTING AT THE DINNER TABLE AND that the platters with the meat, the vegetables, the bread, and all the other trimmings are sitting right in front of the place where someone else is sitting. Now imagine that he serves his own plate, filling up every available inch with whatever there is to eat at that meal. Now imagine that he puts the platters down in the same spot and begins to eat, enjoying the food, smacking his lips, sopping up the gravy with biscuits, and washing it all down with a beverage. Meanwhile, your plate sits empty in front of you. You see the food, and the aroma has long since captivated you. But you have nothing on your plate. What are you likely to say in such a situation? Depending upon just how much religion you really do have, you are at least likely to ask that person to "please pass the platter."

In a sense, the Bread of Life and the Living Water that are the message about Jesus are like that story. We are not meant to fill our plates with the good news of the gospel without being careful to pass it on to others. We are not meant to enjoy the love and grace and forgiveness of God without extending the promise of those things to others. That is the work of salvation – one sinner saved by grace passing on to another the promises of God. D. T. Niles, the Indian preacher of the 1930s and 1940s, described the process this way: "Preaching is one beggar telling another beggar where to find bread." That is the work that Jesus was giving his disciples when he told them to be his witnesses. And that is the work that they have passed down to us today.

It is this issue of passing on to others what we have received that stands at the center of this story in Acts 1:6–8. There is within the structure of the challenge issued by Jesus to his disciples in Acts 1 an internal logic that every congregation, indeed all Christians, must consider as we think about the work that God expects us to do in Christ's name. These words from Jesus come at a critical moment in the life of the still infant Christian community. The earthly ministry of Jesus was over. The work of redemption on the cross at Calvary was complete. The wonder and power of the resurrection had been accomplished. Jesus was about to leave the earth and return to the presence of God in heaven. Before he leaves, however, there is one matter of urgent business that must be resolved. Like a relay runner

---

This sermon was delivered by the author at Antioch Baptist Church in Cleveland, Ohio, on May 5, 1999.

who has to pass the baton on to the person who must run the next leg of the race, Jesus has to pass the baton of earthly ministry on to his disciples. That is the business at hand in these verses in Acts 1.

The disciples had been given two earlier opportunities to go forth and do ministry on their own. The Lord had sent them out two by two and told them to preach the message of grace and salvation, to heal the sick, and to cast out devils in his name. All of this they did, and then they returned to report to him how they had done. That would be the difference this time. In the past, they knew Jesus was not far away. They could look forward to going back to him when their previous two missions were complete. If things did not go well, Jesus would be around to make things work out in the end. But not this time. This time Jesus was leaving the earth. The work of the ministry would become their responsibility.

True enough, the Holy Spirit would provide the power. Jesus tells them explicitly not to do anything until the Holy Spirit comes upon them. They should not go forward in their own wisdom or power. They should not go forward trusting in the assurance that they could do this work on their own. In truth, I have long argued that the book in which these words are found could just as easily have been called "The Acts of the Holy Spirit," for it is the Holy Spirit that is the active agent from beginning to end. However, while the Holy Spirit would have to provide the power, the disciples have to provide the energy and manpower. They would have to make themselves open and available to the movement of the Holy Spirit. That is what Jesus was saying to them. The baton was about to be passed. The salvation history plan of God was hanging in the balance. This was, indeed, a critical moment for the church of Jesus Christ.

There are several things we need to notice in this passage as we in Antioch think about the ministries that we are beginning, on the one hand, and continuing, on the other. Let me list all of them at the outset, and then discuss each one of them in turn. Jesus tells us to:

1. Be his witnesses;
2. Be his witnesses in Jerusalem;
3. Be his witnesses in Judea;
4. Be his witnesses in Samaria;
5. Be his witnesses to the uttermost part of the earth.

It is good that we remind ourselves of these things, so that we do not forget what we as Christians, whether individually or as congregations, are trying to accomplish. We can get so caught up in the "habits" of religion that we lose sight of the objectives that God has set before us. We are not meant to simply fill ourselves up with the Bread of Life and the Living Water. We are to find ways to pass those gifts on.

Notice first of all, that Jesus tells the disciples, "Be witnesses unto me." A danger far too many Christians have fallen into is that of actively pursuing personal salvation but passively responding to the work of ministry. We want to be sure that we have been saved. We want to be sure that our relationship with Christ is secure. But once that has been accomplished, we drop out of the process, not following through to the level where we go from "being saved" to "being witnesses." And yet, this was the critical issue for Jesus. He did not go through the elaborate and miraculous work of incarnation, crucifixion, resurrection, and ascension simply so you and I can be saved as an end in itself. He went through all of that so that we who have been saved by grace can be living witnesses to others of the love and grace and power of God.

God forbid that anybody in this congregation comes here to receive the wondrous knowledge of the grace of God, and not share it with another. God forbid that any member of this congregation come to realize how rich the love of God has been toward you, and then not be willing to display that same love of God toward somebody else. "Be witnesses unto me," says Jesus. Tell those who do not know about the love and mercy of God. Then, let that love flow from us to them in tangible ways that bless their lives, lift their burdens, and encourage their hearts. I say again: you and I are not simply called to be saved. We are also called to be witnesses for the Lord.

I wish you could have been in the church last Thursday at noon. In one area of the building, the laughter of children in the Head Start Center could be heard. In another area, the smell of fried chicken being served at Loaves and Fishes Hunger Center filled the air. Not far away, one of the three groups of Alcoholics Anonymous that meets here was in session. Construction was underway for the Agape Center's HIV/AIDS ministry. In the middle of all of that, several members of the mission society were involved in a quilting circle. From the youngest to the oldest, from the hungry to the recovering alcoholic, and in preparation for those who are struggling with a dreaded disease – the people of God were everywhere, and this building was virtually alive. And no group was wondering why the others were there. All of the activities seemed to have acceptance from all the others.

This is the work to which Jesus calls the church. Not just grand worship services on Sunday, when members drive in from remote locations, stay for a few hours, and then return home. Our work as a congregation continues when all of you go home after the Sunday morning service or the Wednesday evening Bible class, and the resources you generously make available, both financial and facilities, become the means by which the lives of people throughout this community are touched and blessed. This is when the church is most alive, functioning every day of the week, meeting needs at every level – preaching the gospel and displaying the love of God in tangible ways. This is how we are able to meet the challenge of Jesus who says, "Be witnesses unto me."

And be aware that the Greek word used here is the same word used for "martyr." The sense seems to be that we should be witnesses for Christ even in the face of opposition, risk, or danger. We should be prepared to sacrifice, even to suffer, for the sake of Jesus Christ. This is a far cry from the kind of passive religion in which most "Sunday-morning Christians" are engaged. Jesus challenges us to be his "martyrs."

Notice next that Jesus not only advises us on *what* to do, but he also tells us *where* he wants us to go to do the work. He says, "Be witnesses unto me both in Jerusalem, and in all Judea, and in Samaria, and unto the uttermost part of the earth." These are not just four separate locations that Jesus happens to mention at random. These are locations that push us farther and farther away from our comfort zone. Each location pushed those disciples farther away from where they were at the time, and in some cases pushed them into new directions where they did not want to go. Jerusalem was where they stood. It was the city where every Jew wanted to be. To this day, when Jewish people finish their Passover Seder, they read these words with hope and expectation: "Next year in Jerusalem." I am sure that Peter, James, and John would not have minded being witnesses for God in Jerusalem.

Or would they? After all, Jerusalem was where Jesus had been crucified. Jerusalem was where the Palm Sunday crowd changed its tune just four days later and shouted out, "Crucify him!" The disciples were still hiding in the upper room in Jerusalem because they were afraid that, if they showed their faces in the city, they would meet a fate similar to that of Jesus. Remember, when the Holy Spirit fell upon them and gave them boldness, they were gathered in that upper room, still hiding and shaking with fear for their safety. But, Jesus had challenged them to leave the security of that hiding place, to go out into the streets of the city, and "be witnesses unto [him]."

More importantly, Jesus sent his disciples first to the urban center of Jewish life. He did not send them to Bethlehem, Bethany, or Beersheba. He did not send them to Jericho, the vacation resort. He sent them to the big city of Jerusalem. There is an important lesson here for the contemporary American church. With stunning regularity, most Protestant and Catholic churches are moving out of the cities of this nation, seeking safer and more spacious grounds in the suburbs of our society. We see them building their megachurches almost always far removed from the danger zones of the city. They move to places where people who do not have cars cannot reach them. God forbid that public transportation should deliver "those people" to our door. "They" are the reason many churches moved away in the first place.

How do we think we can save our world if we limit our witness to the problems and people of the suburbs? What do we think about Jesus, who sent us first to Jerusalem? What do we think about Paul, who took his message from Antioch to Ephesus to Athens to Corinth to Rome? Paul and Jesus both seemed to understand that society is touched from the core places outward. Any Christian who presumes to make a witness or take a stand for the gospel must ask him or herself what to do about the rotting and forgotten urban centers like Cleveland, Chicago, Boston, Baltimore, New York, and New Orleans. Are these cities not populated with the very people Jesus would point to as the current version of "the least of these"?

The May 4, 1999 edition of the *New York Times* reports that families, businesses, shops and malls, and political influence are all shifting out to the suburbs. What the paper did not report, and what is of even greater consequence for the cause of Jesus Christ, is that churches are also part of this migration from the cities. We need to hear the words of Jesus once again: "Be my martyrs in Jerusalem!"

Then Jesus says to be his witnesses in Jerusalem *and* in Judea. This pushes the work out a little farther. Jerusalem was a city, but Judea was the whole country. Jesus was not just sending his disciples across the street. He was also sending them out to share the gospel with people in the neighboring towns and cities. That takes more time and effort, but it is all a part of passing the platter to others who need and want to eat, and of passing the baton so the work can carry on as God intended. I believe that the Lord is challenging us to stand against the prevailing social values of our nation, and to offer a godly alternative. We should see Judea as the larger region in which Greco-Roman culture and influence was predominant during the days of Jesus. And we should see Judea in our own day as the culture and influence of Hollywood, Wall Street, the Internet, pornographic films and magazines, and violent video games that may have played a role in the death and disaster in Littleton, Colorado. We should not remain isolated while those values dominate the landscape. In the name of Jesus Christ, we need to be witnesses.

This may mean that churches must make more and better use of the very media that concern us most. We can broadcast on radio and TV, and we can have Web pages on the Internet. We may need to be more outspoken on the issues that trouble our society, ranging from gun control to race relations to urban sprawl to the cheap relationships that develop when sex becomes detached from love and marriage.

Clearly, there may be some churches that cannot do this kind of outreach on their own, but that should not prevent them from giving prayerful or financial support to local or national ministries that *can* send the gospel out to a wider circle of listeners. The limited resources of a smaller congregation can be joined together with other caring souls who support the work of agencies such as the United Way, the NAACP, the American Red Cross, Campus Crusade for Christ, or preaching ministries such as the Billy Graham Evangelistic Association. One way or another, every church has been challenged to extend the gospel to Judea.

Now comes the toughest part of the text. Jesus says, "Be witnesses unto me both in Jerusalem, and in all Judea, and in Samaria. . . . " Please note that Samaria was not just another place. The people who lived in Samaria were hated and scorned by the people of Judea. Jews and Samaritans had been feuding and squabbling and hating each other for more than seven hundred years. When Jesus went to a Samaritan village, as recorded in John 4:6 and following, he asked a certain woman to give him a drink of water from Jacob's well. The woman answered with great surprise, "Why do you, a Jew, ask me, a woman of Samaria, to give you a drink? Jews and Samaritans have no dealings with each other." Similarly, the shock of the parable told by Jesus in Luke 10 is that it was a "good *Samaritan*" who stopped to help the beaten Jewish man on the road. In the wake of centuries of hostilities, Jesus was intentionally sending his Jewish followers to spread the love of God in Samaria. What a shock that must have been for them.

Most disciples of Jesus have a direction in which they do not want to go. They have a group of people they do not want to embrace. They have a mission they do not want to embrace. Driven by racism, ethnic rivalries, or blind and ignorant prejudice, there are some people that other people "just don't like." That was the case with the prophet named Jonah. God called him to be a prophet to the nation of Assyria by preaching in their great city of Nineveh. However, Jonah did not want to accept that assignment. Perhaps he did not like "those people." But whatever his reasons were, Jonah took off in the opposite direction, and it required a storm at sea and underwater housing in the belly of a great fish before Jonah finally accepted his mission. Like Jonah, most disciples have a group or a mission they do not want to accept.

This congregation has started a ministry called The Agape Program. It is an education, prevention, and testing program centered on the HIV/AIDS disease. This disease is wiping out whole sections of our community. Black people are 13 percent of the U.S. population, but we are 37 percent of the

HIV/AIDS cases. In Greater Cleveland we account for 63 percent of all reported cases of HIV/AIDS. Contrary to popular opinion, the disease is *not* limited to those who are homosexuals or intravenous drug users. It is at large in the general population, and it is especially threatening to black women and children.

Up to now, all that most churches have done is point fingers, fix blame, and criticize and condemn how some people happened to have contracted this disease. None of that will stop this epidemic that has hit our community. None of that seems to recognize the fact that many people now infected contracted the disease without engaging in any risky behavior. They contracted it from their unfaithful spouse. They contracted it after being raped. Do we simply point our finger at them? And what do we do with the people who have the virus and do not know it, and who may be spreading it as a result of their risky sexual behaviors? We must go to Samaria. Our children are at risk. Spouses who can contract the disease from an unfaithful partner are at risk. The time has come for churches to stop being full of judgment, and start being witnesses to the love of God by showing concern and compassion. As Jesus embraced and worked to heal lepers in his day, so his disciples must work to bring healing and hope to those who have what many consider a modern-day leprosy.

The hope is not simply that persons with AIDS can get into treatment, but also that their families and friends can find support. And just as important, we hope that we can prevent others from contracting this disease if we spread information to the right people before it is too late. We are doing this because we want to be faithful to the challenge from Jesus to be his witnesses, and that requires that we sometimes go into areas where we might not want to go. HIV/AIDS may be one of those areas, but we go there because we have no choice if we are to be faithful to the cause of Jesus Christ.

Finally, the Lord also sends us to be his witnesses "unto the uttermost part of the earth." God is not interested in the salvation of America or the Western Hemisphere or wherever English-speaking nations can be found. In the beginning, God created the heavens and the earth. The song says, "He's got the whole world in his hands." Jesus came so that "whosoever believeth in him should not perish, but have everlasting life." In Acts 1, the church is challenged to go far beyond our comfort zone, to extend ourselves to people who are unlike us in every way, and to make them disciples.

That is why I went to preach last week at the Cleveland Chinese Christian Church. Those were people who had fled communism in their homeland. They came from a nation where the name of Jesus was not often heard, where the church of Jesus still faces oppression and harassment, and where attempting to convert people to faith in Jesus can cost you your life. Despite all of that, these people have found their way to Jesus, and they are supporting programs that help other Chinese people to do the same. What a marvelous experience it was for the forty of us who were there last week.

Many in the congregation could speak little or no English, so the leaders had someone standing right next to me who would translate my words into Mandarin Chinese. Then another a lady in the pastor's office would translate my words into Cantonese, and people wearing special headsets could understand the gospel in that language. That experience reminded me of two objects I spent a lot of time with during my childhood: Crayola crayons and M&M chocolate candies. I shared with those Chinese Christians that I might be different from them on the outside, just like crayons or M&Ms candies look different on the outset. What a wonderful array of colors is found inside both of those packages. However, beneath the surface, beyond color, the crayons and the candies were all the same. Only the outside was different. What they were on the inside, wax crayons or chocolate candies, was exactly the same in taste and texture. And as with crayons and M&Ms, so it is with human beings. We may be different in color, in culture, in custom, in language, and in national origin, but inside we are the same human spirit. And Jesus would have us support any ministry or mission that has as its purpose the spread of the gospel to the uttermost parts of the earth. In so doing, men and women, whatever their color or culture, can be saved. Then, having been saved themselves, they can then pass the baton on to others.

Two weeks ago, I saw the results of what earlier generations of disciples had accomplished by going to the uttermost parts of the earth with the Word of God. I was teaching a class at Ashland Theological Seminary, and three students had been randomly selected to preach that day. As it happened, one was from India, another from Taiwan, and the third from Thailand. Of even greater importance, all three of them were preaching in English for the first time. Obviously they had some difficulties with pronunciation of certain words, enunciation of certain sounds, and with the syntax of some sentences. But that mattered very little in comparison to the power of that afternoon. Students from around Asia were preaching to students from America about their love for Jesus Christ. They had heard about Jesus because somebody took the time to go to the uttermost parts of the earth and spread the gospel.

That was as close as I have yet come to the kingdom of God. We were not gathered there in racial or ethnic isolation, as is so often the case in our churches. It was not all whites over here and all blacks over there. It was not all Baptists here and all others somewhere else. It was not men in the front and women in the back. It was not English-speaking in front and other language groups bringing up the rear. It was a tangible sign of the truth of the song (and the Scripture to which it points) that says:

> How to reach the masses, men of every birth,
> For an answer, Jesus gave a key,
> For I, if I be lifted up from earth,
> Will draw all men unto men.[25]

This is the challenge that awaits every disciple, every congregation that is devoted to the work of Jesus. We must hear and heed the challenge found in Acts 1. We must not be content just to be saved. We must be equally committed to being witnesses. And that work of being a witness for the Lord must begin in the community where we are located and then extend to the farthest reaches of the earth. I believe we are committed to such a ministry here at Antioch. I hope and pray that we will always be willing to go beyond our comfort zone. We must be prepared to be "martyrs" for the cause of Christ. Our commitment must extend even to the point of reaching out to those groups we may not want to embrace, because we want to be faithful to the One who has been gracious to us. And if you have not yet been gripped by this mission, then I challenge you today to respond in faithful obedience to him whose commandment is that we would be his witnesses in Jerusalem, Judea, Samaria, and to the uttermost parts of the earth.

Chapter 3

Preserving History for the Children of the Black Middle Class

Teach them diligently unto thy children.
—*Deuteronomy 6:7, KJV*

W HO KNOWS THE WORDS TO ONE OR MORE VERSES of "Lift Every Voice and Sing"? Who knows the name and ancestry of the wife of the biblical character Moses? Who was the founder of the first black religious denomination in America, and what was the name of that denomination? Who knows that the Underground Railroad is not another name for the New York City subway system? What was the Underground Railroad? What was the Montgomery bus boycott, and what leaders emerged from that event? What nation was linked to the word *apartheid*, and can you name at least one person who struggled to bring that system to an end?

What do you suppose would happen if these questions, and dozens more on the same subject matter, were asked of the children and teens either in the typical middle-class black church or in the neighborhoods where such churches are located? It should be the goal of black middle-class churches to offer a range of learning opportunities in which the history and achievements of black people in a variety of areas can be learned and discussed. Such instruction will prove invaluable when those young people go forth to encounter an American society that is still badly infected with racism.

Why Teach History to Middle-Class Black Youth?

I am greatly informed at this point by the words of Deuteronomy 6:7, in which adults in ancient Israel, and still today at every Passover observance and in every

Hebrew school, are commanded to teach their children diligently about their history and heritage. This would include not only the Ten Commandments and the other religious tenets of their faith but also the history of their years of oppression and slavery: "Beware lest thou forget the Lord, which brought thee forth out of the land of Egypt" (Deuteronomy 6:11, KJV). What does Deuteronomy say now to the black middle class?

This is a time when more and more of the children of the black middle class are being assimilated into mainstream American culture, largely as a result of what they are learning in schools, in the workplace, and in their exposure to pop culture. As a result, there is a great risk that these young black people will never learn about the music, literature, history, and struggles of their own black forebears and contemporaries. Society makes sure they learn about George Washington, but who makes sure they also learn about George Washington Carver? They will certainly learn about Paul Revere and the battle of Lexington and Concord, but who will include the story of Crispus Attucks and the earlier battle of Boston? William Shakespeare is a great playwright, but so too are August Wilson and James Baldwin. While Billy Graham may be the greatest evangelist of the twentieth century, it might be important for black and white students to know about a slave preacher from nineteenth-century Virginia named John Jasper. One of the important ministries of the black middle-class church, especially on behalf of its children and teens, is to "teach them diligently unto thy children."

Opportunities for Teaching Black History in the Church

Among the subject areas that need to be shared are the history of black people in the Western Hemisphere, the history of African people in diaspora around the world (Pan-African studies), and the presence of people of African descent in the Bible. Perhaps the greatest untapped resource is the stories of history makers within a congregation itself, which take the form of oral histories. I will never forget one father-son banquet at Antioch. A member of the famed Tuskegee Airmen, who is a deacon in the church, told us about his early life in Texas and the events that led up to his being trained to be an Army Air Corps bomber pilot with that all-black military unit. Not many days after that, I was speaking to a woman in the receiving line after the morning service who told me how she dated Martin Luther King Jr. when they were students together in Atlanta in the 1940s. Most churches would be surprised to know what historical lessons are seated in their own pews every Sunday.

Talking from the Pulpit and in Sunday School

All of these subject areas can be covered if the pastor and those responsible for the teaching ministry of the church carefully consider all of their opportunities. Some of this can be done in sermons by the pastor who places these topics within the course of a year's preaching. It can also be done through the use of guest speakers who embody some of that history. In July of 1998, Antioch Baptist Church hosted Congressman John Lewis of Georgia, who, along with Martin Luther King Jr., is among the greatest heroes of the civil rights movement. Lewis shared his personal experiences about the freedom rides of 1960–61, the Selma to Montgomery march of 1965, and the tensions between the clergy-led Southern Christian Leadership Conference and the student-led Student Nonviolent Coordinating Committee. After the service, Lewis autographed his book, *Walking with the Wind*, that further discusses these issues.[1] Church leaders would do well to bring these living witnesses to speak to their congregations before they pass from the scene.

Sometimes it is difficult for a local church to attract national figures on its own, but there are other ways to benefit from their expertise and experience. People like C. T. Vivian, Wyatt Tee Walker, Andrew Young, Jesse Jackson, Walter Fauntroy, John Lewis, Marian Wright Edelman, and even Rosa Parks frequently appear at colleges. They are also brought in by foundations and other corporate groups for special programs with the local Urban League or NAACP. With a little planning, and some ongoing networking, many of the living legends of black history can still be made accessible to young people who belong to even the smallest congregations, which could never underwrite such events on their own.

Some of this passing on of the history and culture can be done in Sunday school classes, especially where black characters in the Bible are concerned. I remember seeing Cecil B. DeMille's production of *The Ten Commandments* when I was ten years old. It has never ceased to amaze me that not a single person in ancient Egypt or among the Hebrews, who had lived as slaves in Egypt for over four hundred years, is portrayed in that film as being black or brown. Did all of the people in the Bible really look like Charlton Heston and Yul Brenner?

Scholars, including Cain Hope Felder, and pastors like William McKissick have documented the many passages of Scripture that point to the presence of dark-skinned Africans throughout the biblical story.[2] Those characters would include, but are not limited to, the Ethiopian eunuch; the queen of Sheba; Zipporah the Cushite wife of Moses; Simon of Cyrene, who carried the cross of Jesus; and Simeon called Niger, who was referred to as a prophet in Acts 13. It would be a wonderful exercise to challenge students in Sunday school to identify as many references in the Bible as they can of either dark-skinned or African people.

Teaching through the Ministry of Music. The music ministry of the church affords another opportunity to pass on certain aspects of black history and culture. Whether by the whole congregation, or simply from a choral group, the sacred music history of black people can be incorporated directly into the worship service on an ongoing basis. The emphasis can shift from the spirituals of the slave era, to the early gospel hymns of Thomas A. Dorsey and Charles A.

Tyndale, to the modern arrangements of Andrae Crouch, Richard Smallwood, and Kirk Franklin.

Many young people do not know the history of the spirituals. They are not aware of the double meaning those songs contained, communicating both a spiritual and a protest message.[3] They do not know about the struggles that the early gospel singers faced because many black Christians initially viewed gospel music as so close to the blues that it was deemed inappropriate for use in the church.[4]

Through the ministry of music, young people can discover how many pop artists got their start singing in the church choir. That list includes Nat King Cole, Sam Cooke, Lou Rawls, Aretha Franklin, Gladys Knight, and the Staple Singers. They can learn how groups like Take Six still include sacred music as a part of their regular repertoire. They can learn about the Fisk Jubilee Singers, Roland Carter, Paul Robeson, Marian Anderson, Jessye Norman, and Kathleen Battle, all of whom have helped preserve the spirituals as a valued part of American musical history.

Using Youth-Ministry Events. Some of the lessons of black history can be taught in the various youth-fellowship events that occur throughout the year. Special events like vacation Bible school can offer some of this material as the theme for the one- or two-week program. Over the last few years, Antioch Baptist Church has abandoned the traditional observance of Halloween and has opted for a harvest festival. At this event, the youth from the neighborhood and from the church membership gather for an evening of fun in a safe environment. Instead of dressing as ghosts and vampires, we invite them to come dressed either as biblical characters or as characters out of black history.

The church also sponsors a rites-of-passage program called ORITA, which is a Yoruba word meaning "crossroads." This and other such programs that engage young people between fifteen and seventeen are excellent opportunities to incorporate lessons about American citizenship, Christian discipleship, and an appreciation of African American history and heritage.

Each February is the annual observance of Black History Month. During that time, prizes can be awarded to the persons, youth and adults, who answer a list of questions that need to be researched and then handed in for review. In most years, the church has also sponsored a black film festival during the month. One year the focus may be on the all-black-cast films of the 1920s–40s, such as *Green Pastures*, *Hallelujah*, and *Carmen Jones*. Another year it might focus on issues of racial discrimination, as depicted in *Raisin in the Sun*, *Imitation of Life*, or *Nothing But a Man*. With popcorn, hot dogs, and soda during the movie, and a skilled discussion leader afterward, these have been wonderful occasions for us to "teach them diligently unto thy children."

Teaching through Outreach Ministries. One of the best things a black middle-class congregation can do is directly involve its young people in the outreach ministries of the church. Here is where the lessons about service, charity, self-sacrifice, and Christian discipleship are best taught. Up to now, this chapter has discussed how young people can learn about the achievements and extraordinary efforts of those who came before them. At some point, young people must be challenged to make their own contributions to society.

While contributing themselves is a primary benefit of involving young people in outreach ministry, there is a far more important reason to do so. Black middle-class children who may have lived all their lives in single-family homes and attended quality public, private, or parochial schools in suburban areas have no real appreciation for the plight of the urban poor. They do not know the desolation of many inner-city neighborhoods. They may have viewed such scenes from a passing car as they drove through sections of these areas on their way to church or some downtown destination, but they have never experienced how so many of their peers in the inner city are made to live. The children of the black middle class will not fully appreciate their own life situation, or the efforts required by their families to provide them with that middle-class lifestyle, until they have an opportunity to see, smell, and touch the places that far too many black people call home.

I was raised in the inner city of Chicago in the 1950s and 1960s. I grew up running away from gangs such as the Blackstone Rangers and the Disciples. I heard gunshot sounds in the night. I watched the city of Chicago uproot most of my neighborhood in order to build a highway that would allow commuters to speed through the city. I watched as the most dangerous public-housing units in America were built in Chicago — Stateway Gardens and the Robert Taylor Homes. They stand to this day, eighteen stories tall, lined up one after another for miles along State Street and Wabash Avenue on the city's South Side.

I learned during my childhood the images that were employed by Langston Hughes in his poem "Mother to Son." In it the mother speaks to her son about life as a twisting, dark, splintered stairway that you don't dare stop climbing, no matter how hard the going gets.[5] I grew up in a world described by Alex Kotlowitz in *There Are No Children Here*.[6] This book describes the hazards and horrors encountered every day by two brothers who grew up in another of Chicago's public-housing projects. However, my son and most of the children of our congregation have had no exposure to this world whatsoever. They were all completely disconnected from the suffering and deprivation that many people endured just a short distance from our church.

In two ways, we manage to involve our young people in the outreach ministries of the church so that they could become more familiar with how others are living and more appreciative of how and where they live. Through a partnership with the Cleveland Cavaliers of the National Basketball Association, we have handed out turkeys and bags of other grocery items during the last three Thanksgiving seasons. Our young people have been the ones actually giving the items to the hundreds of families who come to claim one of those gift baskets. We also involve the young people in Project Angel Tree, which is a program that provides gifts and a party for approximately two hundred children who have a parent incarcerated during the Christmas season. Handing out these gifts and realizing how many children fall into this category combine to be a sobering experience for our young people. In both instances, this is a life that most, if not all, of the young people in our church have never known and have barely noticed.

When a family is not able to attend the Project Angel Tree affair, it is our practice to have members of our church deliver the gifts to them. My son and I were assigned to deliver the gifts to a family at their home in one of Cleveland's oldest public-housing units, Garden Valley Estates. My son had never been to a public-housing project. He had never walked up one of those narrow, unlit stairwells that smelled of urine and had gang signs scrawled along the walls and hallways. Having walked up three flights of stairs, we arrived at the door of the family we had come to visit. When the door opened, we were nearly overcome by the heat from the stove on which the mother was cooking soul food. The young woman, whose husband was in prison, was raising three children in that cramped and stuffy apartment. They received our gifts with much appreciation. However, during our ride home, my son was as quiet as I have ever seen him. You could tell that he was trying to come to grips with his encounter with a world he had never seen, smelled, or felt before. Our young people need to have a hands-on experience with such outreach ministries. It is one of the best ways we can "teach them diligently unto thy children."

The Challenges of Learning Black History in American Society

Black people have a great story to tell about our endurance in the face of unimaginable oppression. It extends from the Middle Passage, which began forcibly exporting Africans to the European colonies of the West in the fifteenth century, through slavery, which stretched over 250 years in the Americas, through the Jim Crow system, which continues to this day. Despite this ordeal, black people still produced a wide variety of genius, ranging from Garrett Morgan to Madame C. J. Walker to Hiram Revels to Mary McLeod Bethune. There is no more poignant story than the performance at the 1936 Olympic Games in Berlin of Jesse Owens, which shattered Adolf Hitler's propaganda about Aryan superiority. These are stories that we must diligently teach to our children.

By and large, America has not been interested in telling this story or preserving this history. It has only been in the last decade that Hollywood films and television programs, college reading lists, museum exhibitions, and the repertoire of performing arts groups have included the history and contributions of black people. There is one national holiday devoted to an African American hero —

Martin Luther King Jr. Day. However, as with all other American holidays, that day is already becoming just another opportunity to stay in bed or go browsing in the mall at a sale on clothes or furniture.

In a sudden shift from teaching history solely through the eyes of whites in America, most elementary and secondary schools now offer a multicultural curriculum. This does not mean that more attention is now given to the achievements and contributions of black people in America and around the world. Instead, it means that black history and culture are taught alongside the equally compelling stories of the many and varied Hispanic and Native American groups, whose stories have also been left largely untold by the purveyors of American culture. Our children also need to know about the historic struggles of Jewish people, both before and after the Holocaust. And given the emergence of the Pacific Rim as a major engine in the world's economy, they need to know as much as possible about the languages, cultures, and history of the people of Southeast Asia.

All of these stories must be told, but the atmosphere is one in which scholars like Arthur Schlesinger Jr. and E. D. Hirsch warn us about the loss of our national identity as Americans if we spend too much time in pursuit of our individual ethnic heritage.[7] However, the need still exists to teach our children about their own history and heritage. Further it seems increasingly less likely that this instruction will take place in the public schools, where most children of the black middle class are enrolled, because there the emphasis has already shifted to multicultural instruction, a practice with which I have no objections whatsoever. It is even less likely that any meaningful black history or culture will be acquired by those increasing numbers of black middle-class students who are enrolled in the private and parochial schools of our nation. (As I mentioned in chapter 2, many parents who struggle to pay the tuition for their children to attend those schools are often shocked by the racial insensitivity they find among teachers and administrators alike.)

The Black Church as an Appropriate Place to Teach History

Enter the black middle-class church. An opportunity exists in that setting to "teach them diligently unto thy children." There is an urgency with which the black church, especially the middle-class churches, needs to answer this call to action. Such churches have the financial resources to provide access to the books, films, and other teaching tools that would be necessary. In most instances, there are within the membership of such churches persons who already possess great expertise and familiarity with this subject matter. There are probably several schoolteachers in the congregation of most black middle-class churches in such areas as social studies, music, arts and crafts, and literature. Such persons can be helpful in a number of ways. They can either help provide instruction, work in teacher training for others who will work with the children, or work with church leaders in the design of an overall program of study. They may know how to secure certain materials at little or no cost to the church.

In the church, there are no limitations that can be imposed upon the curriculum by any accreditation agency. There is no need to allocate time for the study of other ethnic groups as an act of political correctness, even though I would recommend that other cultures be taught as a matter of providing balance and perspective.

Teaching about the Historic Role of the Church. Given the central role the church has played in the black community for the last two hundred years, it makes perfect sense for the church to teach its youth about its own historic importance. For example, many slave rebellions of the nineteenth century were planned in black churches, and with the full knowledge and consent of the pastors of those churches.[8] Aldon Morris, in *Origins of the Civil Rights Movement*, points out that the modern civil rights movement of the 1950s and 1960s grew directly out of the black church.[9] Charles Hamilton, in *The Black Preacher in America*, contends that for the foreseeable future the black church will continue to be the most influential institution in most black communities.[10]

Teaching about the Link between the Black Church and Education. We must teach our children about the close connection between the black church and a host of educational institutions and the notable individuals affiliated with them. They need to know about Bishop Daniel Payne. In addition to being a leader in the African Methodist Episcopal Church in the 1850s, he was also the first black person to serve as a college president in American history when he was appointed president of Wilberforce College in Ohio in 1856.[11] They need to know about the many historically black colleges throughout the country that began as church-sponsored institutions. They need to know about Mordecai Johnson, a Baptist minister who was the first black president of Howard University. They need to know about Benjamin Mays at Morehouse College and Samuel Proctor at Virginia Union, who were both active clergymen and college presidents.[12] They need to see that this church involvement continues through Rev. William Gray III, a Baptist pastor who also serves as head of the United Negro College Fund.

Our young people need to learn about Mary McLeod Bethune, founder of Bethune Cookman College in Daytona Beach, Florida, and her list of things that she expressed as her legacy to all black people:

> I leave you love — I leave you hope — I leave you the challenge of developing confidence in one another — I leave you a thirst for education — I leave you a respect for the use of power — I leave you faith — I leave you racial dignity — I leave you a desire to live harmoniously with your fellow men — I leave you, finally, a responsibility to our young people.[13]

The church can take responsibility for our young people by passing along such wisdom as this from the founder of a great black college.

Training Our Youth to Respond to Racism

It is important for black middle-class youth to be taught their own history and culture because no matter where they go, they will continue to face racism on the one hand and assimilation and acculturation on the other. They need confidence that their own culture and heritage are worth preserving, no matter how it is demeaned by some or seems to be overshadowed by others. Such was in evidence at Dartmouth College, where a group of white students sponsored a "ghetto party" on the campus of that elite Ivy League institution: "They were dressed as gangsta rap artists, some sporting Afro wigs and carrying toy guns." This shocking event followed a mock slave auction, which was sponsored as a fund-raiser by one of Dartmouth's sororities. All this provoked a black student at the college to say, "I live in a ghetto. For Dartmouth students to mock a situation I was lucky enough to get out of by the grace of God just seems to me to be very snooty and very arrogant."[14]

Black students can, and may, escape the ghettos of America and arrive on Ivy League campuses like Dartmouth. Escaping the racism that is so pervasive in American society is another matter, and much more difficult to achieve. It is important for young black middle-class people to know that racism is as prevalent on elite college campuses as it is in urban ghettos and barrios. Black people do not escape racism in America; they simply experience racism in different forms and locations, based upon their socioeconomic level. And based upon their educational level, black people may cope with and respond to racism in different ways. The church can equip young black people to do this.

Let me recap the kind of lessons the church can teach black middle-class students in order to equip them to confront and respond to the kinds of events that occurred at Dartmouth in 1998. A broad awareness of African American history and culture equips young black people to dismiss the racist claims and comments made by whites who seem to infer white superiority. An awareness that other groups, including white groups, have been the targets of systematic, institutional oppression allows young black people to feel less targeted and / or victimized when such events take place. Getting black middle-class youth involved in meeting the needs of those families in the black underclass helps the middle-class youth to put in perspective whatever racist encounters they may have experienced. All things being considered, the black middle class in general, and the young people of that group, do not experience racism in the same ways as do their counterparts in the public-housing units of the urban North or the rural counties of the Deep South. But there is no place in America where a black person will not face some form of racial bigotry and discrimination. Given this reality, it is probably better to have your encounter with racism occur while a student at Dartmouth, or any of the other elite colleges in which many young black people are enrolling these days, than to be limited to low-paying jobs or possibly be drawn into the welfare or criminal-justice systems due to a lack of education and marketable skills.

Finally, black middle-class youth will likely be more inclined toward interracial dating and marriage than their parents and grandparents were, or were allowed to be. The more freely they move within the American mainstream, be it workplace or college campus, the more likely it is that they will meet and mingle with persons of the opposite sex of a different racial background. Will these young people feel the need to avoid these relationships, or keep them hidden, because they believe their parents and families will not be supportive? I know many black people who delight to observe that Moses married outside his race when he chose to marry a Cushite woman named Zipporah.

How should we respond today when our best and brightest young people decide to reach across racial and ethnic lines to find a friend or a spouse? I am not advocating that interracial dating and marriage should happen to any greater degree. I am only suggesting that they probably will among black middle-class youth because they will be moving within the mainstream of American society sooner, more frequently, and for a longer portion of their lives than any previous generation of black youth. What will we diligently teach them about this matter? What are the things we especially want them to know and to do in this area? This, too, must be a part of what is involved when we "teach them diligently unto thy children."

The Year 2000 and Beyond

In his book *The Young Negro in America 1960–1980*, Samuel Proctor attempted to lay out the challenges and opportunities that the middle-class black youth of that era would encounter. Proctor starts with the sit-ins that erupted on black college campuses in 1960 and attempts to project what black youth will need to do to be successful in a world that would be forever different from the one in which Proctor himself had grown up. His advice came within four brilliant chapters that challenged young black people to

1. reverse the spiral toward futility
2. overcome the deficits in education
3. break the cycle of poverty
4. outlive the stereotypes[15]

As surely as Proctor watched his children grow up in a world vastly different from the one in which he grew up, and yet offered them seasoned wisdom on how to be successful, the same process must be repeated today. My son has grown up in a world of fax machines, modems, the Internet, e-mail, the global village, and ATM cards, which allow you to receive cash anywhere around the world by simply punching in the right sequence of numbers or letters. My son, Aaron, would be as bored by the world in which his mother and I grew up as we are left breathless in our attempts to keep up and catch up with his world, which seems always to be changing.

One of the most significant changes since Proctor's 1966 book is the fact that more and more black middle-class students are attending predominantly white colleges instead of the historically black schools that played a much larger role in the college options of previous generations of black college students. An article in the January 1999 issue of *Black Enterprise* reports this change. In addition to traditional locations such as Morehouse College, Spelman College, and Florida A&M University, many black students are now attending such predominantly white schools as Florida State University and Amherst College in Massachusetts.[16]

It is especially important that students attending these colleges be exposed to aspects of black history and culture in their churches because it is less likely they will be exposed to much of it on white college campuses. However, given the continued strength of so many of the historically black colleges and universities, as the *Black Enterprise* article clearly demonstrates, one of the things that parents might well consider is directing their children to consider one of those schools. They are a wealth of history in and of themselves, as far as their founders and alumni are concerned. Moreover, they also provide students with an environment in which they can gain a quality education and also be further exposed to multiple aspects of black history and culture.

There is much seasoned wisdom that can be passed on from the parents' generation to the generation of their children, and the church is an ideal setting for that transfer of knowledge and values to occur. This chapter has attempted to lay out what some of those lessons might be for young people who will reach their adulthood in the twenty-first century. Let us be sure that we "teach them diligently unto our children."

What Shall We Teach Our Children?

Deuteronomy 6

NO ISSUE SEEMS TO HAVE BECOME AS CONTROVERSIAL within the African American community as deciding whether or not to talk to our children about the sad and painful history of our people in this country. How much, if anything at all, should we tell them about the social and political conditions faced by their parents, grandparents, and even more distant forebears? For the longest time, black people have not wanted to talk about the years we spent in slavery or under the restrictions of Jim Crow laws. It is as if we have been too ashamed of that episode and have not wanted to think about it, much less talk about it with our children.

This feeling is as old as the birth of the first generation of black people born after slavery, in the reconstruction era. Belinda Hurmece has edited a collection of twenty-one oral histories of people who actually lived through slavery, entitled, *My Folks Don't Want Me to Talk about Slavery*. In the introduction, she reports on the comments of Sarah Debro, who had been a slave in North Carolina. Sarah reports that her parents told her never to talk about slavery because they were ashamed of having lived in that condition. That feeling did not end with Sarah Debro's generation. It has persisted from that time until now. There are many black people who, like the parents of Sarah Debro, believe, "We aren't the ones to blame for slavery. Why talk about it now?"

As we stand at the dawn of another century and a new millennium, it seems useful to visit this question again. What should we teach our children about the history and experiences of their ancestors in this country? The question is made all the more urgent, because this is literally the first generation that has no living memory of and no conscious experience with the kind of racism and blatant discrimination that was once the norm in this country. Our children were born after the deaths of Martin Luther King Jr., Malcolm X, Fannie Lou Hamer, and Medgar Evers. The Civil Rights Movement, which was the event through which my generation of black Americans has lived, is little more to them than a chapter in a history book.

They never experienced the humiliation of posted signs that read *WHITE* and *COLORED*. They were never required to sit in the back of a bus or at the front of a train where the noise and fumes were the worst. In this

---

This sermon was preached by the author at the Children's Day service at Antioch Baptist Church in Cleveland, Ohio, on June 13, 1999.

age of Denzel Washington and Will Smith, they have never had the experience of either never seeing a black face on a motion picture screen, or if there was a black character, seeing that person was always a slave, a buffoon, or a criminal. This generation of black children has always attended integrated public schools, often with black people serving as principals of the buildings. They watched General Colin Powell lead United States military forces in the Persian Gulf War. They are aware that black people across this country hold thousands of political offices at every level of government.

Noted black intellectual Michael Eric Dyson attempted to discuss what he saw as the stereotypes he identified in a character in the recently released film, *Star Wars: The Phantom Menace*. Most of the youth of this generation either did not know what he was talking about, or they simply did not care. Prior to the 1950s, the stereotyping of black people was not an occasional practice in a limited number of films. It was the standard practice in films, television, radio, cartoons, novels, and commercial advertisements. But, the young people of this generation have no recollection of those days when blacks were depicted, in the language of Donald Bogle, as *Toms, Coons, Mulattoes, Mammies*, and *Bucks.*

Perhaps now is the time to leave all the pain and hardship of our history behind us. Maybe our children are better off if we simply let them enjoy the world in which they now live, and not keep trying to tell them about the world in which previous generations of our people had to exist. Should we keep talking about sharecropping, the Great Migration away from poverty, the staggering rate of lynch-mob justice all over the country? Should we keep talking about segregation in every area of American life, public and private? Should we keep alive the names of *Plessy v. Ferguson*, Emmett Till, Nat Turner, and Harriet Tubman? What should we teach our children about our history in this country?

I believe there is much that can be gained if we take a look at how Israel handled this same problem in Deuteronomy 6. They, too, had once been slaves and for a longer period of time than slavery existed in North America. For four hundred and thirty years Israel was enslaved by the pharaohs of Egypt. During those years, the Hebrew slaves built the great cities, statues, and monuments of Egypt. And for a certain period of time, when their time of enslavement was drawing to a close, they even had to make bricks without straw. However, in Deuteronomy 6, when the Hebrews set out to provide a history lesson for their children, they did not avoid the episode about slavery. They did not simply stop there. They acknowledged that they had indeed been slaves, but they quickly moved on to say that now they were living in a good and abundant land. They had been slaves, but they had come a long way since that time. And in making that observation, the Hebrews were saying a lot about themselves and about God.

I believe that we should teach our history to our children, no matter how painful or shameful it may have been at the time. They may never fully appreciate the benefits and opportunities they now enjoy if they do not also understand that things have not always been as they are today. Last week I participated in the commencement ceremony at Shaker Heights High School. I also signed every one of the diplomas because I am the president of the local school board. None of that was possible when I finished high school in 1966. There were no black members on the Chicago Board of Education in 1966.

I sat there and listened to the senior class president and the student body president, both of them black, address the hundreds of people who had gathered for that ceremony. I remembered as I sat there that, when my mother graduated as the valedictorian of her Chicago high school class in 1932, no black student had been allowed to participate in the ceremony in any way. It is apparent, in fact, wherever I look, that the world in which my son now lives is almost incomprehensible to my mother, and the world in which my mother once lived is nearly impossible for my son to imagine. This is an important story for us to tell.

Notice in the text in Deuteronomy that the writer not only acknowledged that the Hebrews had been slaves in Egypt. The writer also acknowledged that things had changed dramatically. The people now lived in their own land, and they were the masters of their own fates. Slaves were who they had been, but slaves they were no longer. And we as African Americans need to learn from this and start taking careful note of the many and marvelous ways in which our lives have drastically and dramatically improved. And even though it is true that not all black people have progressed as far or as fast as some among us, the general improvement in the lives of black people in America simply cannot be ignored. We need to avoid so focusing on the aspects of racism and bigotry that remain, that we fail to see the achievements that have been made over the last few decades, and the opportunities that are now available.

As a single example, I wonder how many of our young people – who are always searching for role models among the ranks of athletes, rap singers, and movie stars – have decided to hang a picture of Kenneth Chenault on the wall of their bedroom or dorm room? I wonder how many black *adults* even know the name of Kenneth Chenault? We all know about Kirk Franklin, Michael Jordan, Shaquille O'Neal, Puff Daddy, and others of that group of superstar athletes and entertainers. But what about Kenneth Chenault? He is the man who has just been named the next chief executive officer of American Express, one of the largest financial service companies in the world. He has been in charge of their credit card business for the last several years. He is the man who oversees the green, gold, and platinum card about which we are told, "Don't leave home without it." And he is just one of the many black people who now hold leadership positions, not only in public agencies and governmental bodies but in corporate America as well. We have come a long way.

The Surgeon General of the United States is a black man named David Satcher, who went to medical school right here in Cleveland and attended this church during his student years. The president of the American League, which embraces one-half of the teams comprising major-league baseball, is a black man named Leonard Coleman from Montclair, New Jersey, whom I knew when I served a church in that town. Robert Johnson has turned the Black Entertainment Network into a powerhouse in the cable TV industry. Cornel West, Henry Louis Gates Jr., Orlando Patterson, and William Julius Wilson have created an African American studies department at Harvard University that is unparalleled anywhere in the world. None of this should be construed as my suggestion that all of our problems have passed away. However, we will find the courage and energy to consider the struggles that still lie ahead of us when we take note of the accomplishments and achievements that have been made as a result of the struggles of the past. Like the Hebrews, we were slaves, but – ! *This* is what we must teach our children.

However, it is important that we tell our children more than what we have been able to achieve in our lifetime, dramatic though those achievements have been. Part of what we must also tell our children is that we expect them to do much more with their lives than we could have ever accomplished in ours. We must challenge them, not just to focus in on the opportunities that presently exist but to set their sights on the doors that are not yet open and to knock them down or swing them open. Just as the generation ahead of mine expected us to go further than they did, we must do the same with each successive generation. When Joshua led the people of Israel into the Promised Land, how could they have ever imagined the power and splendor that would emerge under the reign of David and Solomon? When Jefferson, Franklin, and Washington began shaping a new nation in 1776, how could they have imagined the economic and technological might of the country today? If successive generations had not improved upon and exceeded the achievements and aspirations of their forebears, they would have been considered low-achievers at best, failures at worst. We dare not set a lower standard for ourselves.

Every black adult needs to challenge and encourage some black youngster to be a success in some area of endeavor. We cannot allow them to become comfortable with the tired old excuses of what white people will not let them do. White people did not *let* Mary McLeod Bethune begin a college in Daytona Beach, Florida, at the turn of the twentieth century. She just did it! White people did not *let* Daniel Hale Williams perform the first successful open-heart surgery at Provident Hospital in Chicago in 1893; he just did it. All that white people did for Jackie Robinson in 1947 was give him the chance to play baseball in the major leagues. Everything that he achieved, both on the field and off, he did on his own. White people did not *let* Paul Robeson become among the greatest athletes, singers, actors, and social activists in American history. He just did all of those things – in one lifetime. We must become increasingly impatient with excuses and increasingly demanding of achievement and results. That is what our parents demanded of us, and that is what we must demand of our children. This is certainly a part of what we must tell them.

What is equally important is that we adults be willing to make whatever sacrifices are necessary to allow our children to take advantage of the opportunities that now exist for them. We all know that traveling outside of the country is a great way to grow and mature as human beings. I had never left this country until I went on my honeymoon at the age of twenty-six, and even then I only went to the Caribbean. One generation later, my son had the opportunity to travel to Europe with his high school marching band when he was fourteen, and to Central Asia with a national wrestling team when he was seventeen. It required some sacrifice on his parents' part to get him on both of those trips. However, that was nothing compared to what my mother sacrificed to provide me with opportunities when I was growing up, including putting me through college at great expense to her own needs and wants. But that was done for so many of us who are now adults, and that is what we should be ready and willing to do for our children today.

The final thing that parents must teach their children is the truth about how we made it from the dark days of slavery until now. That is another major point being made in Deuteronomy 6. God tells Israel to remember that it was not their efforts, but God's grace and power that brought them out of their slavery in Egypt. We must tell the same story to our children. It was not by any efforts of our own, but by the grace of God that we have come this far. Why was slavery not able to destroy our spirits, if not our bodies? Why was Jim Crow unable to break our determination to achieve full and equal citizenship? Why were evil men like "Bull" Connor in Birmingham, Jim Clark in Selma, Ross Barnett in Mississippi, and Lester Maddox in Georgia unable ultimately to deprive us of our hopes and dreams? While we should never underestimate the work and courage of our leaders like Dr. King, Septima

Clark, Malcolm X, and others, we dare not overlook the fact that, as the song says, "We've come this far by faith, leaning on the Lord."

This point was made in a powerful way in a recent story in the [Cleveland] Plain Dealer last week. A national study was done to determine what sources of support were most mentioned by elderly black women who have lived most of their lives in poverty. When the findings were reported, the local religion editor called me to see if the report seemed consistent with my experience. He was actually quite surprised by what had been reported. The majority of the women answered that they were able to endure the hardships of their lives because of their deep and abiding faith in God. Over and over again, these women stated that they could bear their burdens, endure their hardships, and face their problems because they knew they were not alone. They firmly believed that their faith would see them through it all.

What that report did not conclude is that one generation after another of our people has reached the same conclusion. That is the message in the great song, "Lift Every Voice and Sing." One verse says:

> God of our weary years,
> God of our silent tears,
> Thou who has brought us thus far along the way...

In Deuteronomy 6, it was made clear to Israel that they should not boast about what they had done for themselves. Instead, they should acknowledge that God had delivered them with "great signs and wonders." So it is with us today. God has delivered us with great signs and wonders. When the NAACP successfully challenged segregation in public schools and had Plessy v. Ferguson overturned, ending more than one-half century of de jure second-class status for black people, that was a great sign and wonder. When the Montgomery Bus Boycott, in the face of threats and intimidation, was able to get more than 90 percent of all black people to avoid the buses for 381 days, that was a great sign and wonder. When young black students found the courage to withstand centuries of segregation and dared to integrate schools, lunch counters, and bus terminals – those actions were great signs and wonders. When the 1964 Civil Rights Act and the 1965 Voting Rights Act were signed into law, finally providing the freedom and opportunities that America had denied her black citizens since the end of the Civil War, those were great signs and wonders. As a result of those two laws, as Jesse Jackson says so graphically, "Hands that once picked cotton now pick presidents and members of Congress." That, too, is a great sign and wonder.

These things we must teach our children. First, that we were slaves. There is no shame in that statement, so long as it is followed by a comma and not a period. The all-important second point is this: that we are slaves no longer. We as a people have come a long way since we labored in bondage. Third, we have every right to expect our children to aspire to things that were unimaginable in our generation. And we ought to be willing to sacrifice to help them reach their goals. And most important of all, we should never lose sight of the fact that we have not managed to accomplish any of this on our own.

> We've come this far by faith,
> Leaning on the Lord,
> Trusting in His Holy Word,
> He's never failed [us] yet.[17]

Chapter 4

Black Middle-Class Churches as Change Agents

You are the salt of the earth.

—*Matthew 5:11*

ESUS' IMAGE OF THE DISCIPLES AS "THE SALT OF THE EARTH" is an excellent analogy for considering the ministry possibilities of black middle-class churches in inner-city communities. More than any other institution in these communities, black middle-class churches are uniquely positioned to provide a wide range of services, programs, and resources to a population that otherwise might not be served.

In the ancient Near East, salt was not used to season food simply in order to enrich the taste. More importantly, salt was a preservative that prolonged the life of food and helped to delay, if not avoid, its decay. Salt was an absolute essential for life in that region in those days. By using the analogy of the church as the salt of the earth, Jesus was clearly challenging his disciples to enrich the quality of life for the people who come into contact with them.

What better way is there to view the ministry of black middle-class churches in inner-city areas than as agents that both prolong life and help to avoid decay in communities where almost every other business and institution have abandoned the area? In some respects, churches are among the very few institutions that have remained in the inner city. A drive through any of America's inner-city communities will reveal that barber shops and beauty parlors, bars and package good stores, a wide assortment of small businesses, and churches of various sizes occupy almost every corner, amid a sea of vacant lots and abandoned buildings.

This flight from the inner cities has resulted in the loss of a tax base, the rapid decline in the size of the middle class remaining in the cities, and the relocation of most of the neighborhood conveniences that people in the suburbs take for granted. Almost everything that inner-city residents need in order to have a meaningful life are located outside their communities, ranging from medical care to adequate shopping facilities to employment beyond minimum-wage jobs in fast-food restaurants. Those services that have not yet moved out are priced higher than in other areas, supposedly to compensate for increased costs for insurance, security, and theft. Thus, double jeopardy exists for people already impoverished and required to pay more for everything from bread to gasoline to Pampers.

These communities have become engulfed in drugs, crime, gangs, and poverty. They are already in a state of emergency, and there are not many quarters from which help can come. It is into this setting that the church needs to respond to the challenge from Jesus to be the salt of the earth. The churches occupied by members of the black middle class are located precisely in the areas where the need for a helping hand is the greatest. It would be unconscionable for the fairly secure members of these churches to gather once or twice a week for worship and fellowship among themselves and not find effective and creative ways to respond to the socioeconomic needs that are found just outside the door of their churches.

Woe to Those at Ease

Black middle-class churches in inner-city areas must be careful that the words of the prophet Amos not be directed at them: "Woe to them that are at ease in Zion" (Amos 6:1, KJV). This eighth-century prophet of Israel was condemning the leisure class of his nation for living well, eating the choicest cuts of meat, drinking the best wines, living in luxurious homes, and anointing themselves with the most expensive fragrances. All this they do "but are not grieved over the ruin of Joseph" (Amos 6:6, NRSV).

Over and over, Amos condemns Israel for being so focused on how well some people were living; the nation was not interested in the plight of the most disadvantaged. As a result, the prophet clearly states that the suffering Israel would soon experience at the hands of the Assyrians, and later at the hands of the Babylonians, is the result of the lack of compassion that well-to-do members of Israelite society showed toward those who were in greatest need.

A New Testament analogy for the same problem is the parable of the rich man and Lazarus in Luke 16:19–31. This story cuts even closer to the core of the issue because it speaks about poverty that sits just outside the door. It speaks about destitution that is not unseen; it is just overlooked. It speaks about human need that is not unknown; it is just ignored. Unless black middle-class churches in these inner-city communities respond with compassion and with substance to "the ruin of Joseph" and the "poor man named Lazarus" (Luke 16:20, NRSV), we stand condemned by both Amos 6 and Luke 16.

James Cone, in an essay in *The Pastor as Servant*, quotes from a statement that circulated at a poor people's rally in Albuquerque, New Mexico. The statement warned that churches must guard against responding to pressing problems in their own vicinity with little more than pious words. It says:

> I was hungry
> and you formed a humanities club
> and you discussed my hunger.
> Thank you.
>
> I was imprisoned
> and you crept off quietly
> to your chapel in the cellar
> and prayed for my release.
>
> I was naked
> and in your mind
> you debated the morality of my appearance.
>
> I was sick
> and you knelt and thanked God
> for your health.
>
> I was homeless
> and you preached to me
> of the spiritual shelter of the love of God.
>
> I was lonely
> and you left me alone
> to pray for me.
> You seem so holy;
> so close to God.
>
> But I'm still very hungry
> and lonely
> and cold.
>
> So where have your prayers gone?
> What have they done?
> What does it profit a man
> to page through his book of prayers
> when the rest of the world is crying for his help?[1]

The Church as the Salt of the Earth

How can black middle-class churches respond to the needs that exist just beyond their walls, ones that often present themselves at the door on any given day of the week? If properly organized and motivated, churches can possibly mean the difference between life and death for many people and families in the surrounding area. Black middle-class churches located in America's inner cities can fulfill the mandate from Jesus by being engaged in such areas as

1. social services
2. economic development; land acquisition and development
3. credit unions and financial-management seminars
4. education from pre-K through twelfth grade
5. health and wellness
6. voter registration and education
7. civil rights advocacy
8. traditional spiritual programs open and available to the community

I mention these areas of activity, not as random suggestions of things that pastors and churches might want to attempt to implement, but rather as some of the areas in which black middle-class congregations operating in the same general vicinity in Cleveland are presently engaged. Here are working models of how the ministry of the church in the inner city can occur.

All of the churches mentioned in this chapter are members of the same ministerial alliance, United Pastors in Mission. Working together, instead of competing against one another, these churches have a collective ministry that is having a tremendously positive impact in the Fairfax, Mt. Pleasant, Central, and Hough communities on the east side of Cleveland, Ohio. However, what we are doing, individually and collectively, can be replicated in any inner-city area in the United States.

It is important to note at the outset of this discussion that the precise manner in which the church can be involved will vary from one instance to the next. Sometimes the church opens its doors to allow certain programs to operate inside the building; however, the actual expertise required to operate those programs may or may not reside within the congregation. Sometimes the programs occur elsewhere in the community, but the church can help either by providing staff assistance and / or volunteers or by agreeing to underwrite the expenses of that program through financial support from its missions budget. In some cases, the church uses its moral authority or its political influence to advance certain issues that benefit those who live in the surrounding community. Finally, there may be members of the church who have a certain skill and expertise that is needed. This might involve such areas of expertise as medicine, the law, and education and a host of manual talents. The church must challenge its own members to step forward and be willing to offer their time and talents, often on a pro bono basis.

Sometimes the church is represented by the involvement of the pastor, or another clergyperson serving on the staff, who sits on the board of a community agency that directs services to the people who live near the church. Other times, it is the lay members of the church who step forward to provide that civic leadership and support. It is incumbent upon the pastor in these churches to not let the congregation off the hook by doing all of the public ministry himself or herself. I have seen congregations that took great delight in the involvement of the pastor but felt no personal obligation to get involved and lend a helping hand.

The point is that there are many ways and many locations in which the black middle-class church can be the salt of the earth for the neighborhood in which it is located. The more of these areas in which a local church is involved, the deeper into the life of that community will their salt penetrate. And when the ministry involvements of one local church are planned with an awareness of what neighboring congregations are doing in the community, there is a greater chance of covering more areas of need, as opposed to duplicating programs.

The first step in this process of being the salt of the earth may involve challenging the congregation to see and seize the vision of service right in its own backyard. These churches may be inclined to think about missions and service in global and national terms, rather than looking within the immediate environs of the church building. They may be more than willing to be generous and responsive, but they might not yet be thinking about such outreach occurring in areas closer to home. For instance, when Hurricane Mitch devastated the Central American nations of Honduras, Nicaragua, and El Salvador, I saw black middle-class churches in Cleveland, and across the country, respond with remarkable compassion and generosity. Our own congregation sent $5,000 through the American Red Cross, and our clergy alliance responded with another $15,000. However, while missions in faraway places have always been an important part of the life of the church, we must respond with equal compassion and generosity to the crises that occur every day right in our own backyard.

All of this is consistent with the teaching of 1 John 3:18, which challenges the church by saying, "Little children, let us love, not in word or speech, but in truth and action" (NRSV). The sermon "Disciplines for Discipleship," which is found at the end of this chapter, speaks to the spiritual preparation that must first occur within a congregation if it is to respond to the needs and challenges that exist in the inner-city areas where the church is located.

Social Services

One of the most meaningful and effective roles the church can play is that of host to a variety of agencies that deliver social services to residents in the community. Groups such as Alcoholics Anonymous (AA) and Narcotics Anonymous (NA) are always in need of facilities in which to meet because most clients attempt to attend a meeting on a daily basis. Many of them are required to attend meetings as part of a parole or probation agreement with the court system. To have several meeting places scattered throughout the community is a great convenience.

Antioch Baptist Church hosts three AA groups—on Tuesday evening, Thursday morning, and Saturday afternoon. Several other churches in the area also host these programs.

Another service that is becoming increasingly important in inner-city areas involves providing food to needy and homeless families. The church might operate a food pantry for persons who have the means to prepare food for themselves. Or the church might finance and staff a hunger center, which cooks and serves meals in the church. This is one of the ways that church members can have a hands-on experience in ministry. At Antioch we call our food ministry Loaves and Fishes. The hunger center serves a hot lunch on Tuesday and Thursday afternoons and a hot dinner on Monday evenings. We host this ministry, which is sponsored by the ecumenical agency East Side Interfaith Ministry. Our church serves the Monday dinner on a rotating basis with a suburban Episcopal congregation, a group of Jewish students in a Hillel Center at Case Western Reserve University, and an association of black police officers. The Antioch Mission Society, consisting largely of older women, also prepares sandwiches and hot soup for the Thursday lunches.

In order to be sure that as many people in the church as possible get involved in Loaves and Fishes, we assign people to serve during their birth month. Thus, persons born during the month agree to cook the food, serve the plates, and fellowship with the people who have come to the church for that much-needed meal. Many other areas of church involvement are also assigned during members' birth months. Thus, while they may be extremely busy for that one month, they are virtually relieved of any further obligation for the balance of the year. Yet, the ministry of the church continues because members born in the upcoming month pick up the work and carry on. We have a year-round ministry without wearing out a handful of loyal workers.

Economic Development, Land Acquisition and Development

While the need for a wide range of social services will always exist in inner-city communities, black middle-class churches can and should do more than just apply bandages to increasingly cancerous wounds. One of the areas in which more and more churches are becoming involved, either alone or in alliance with other agencies and congregations, is economic development. By this I mean actions that result in improving the economic viability of the community and the people who live there. This would include such activities as creating jobs, developing housing, and helping to guide banks that are responding to The Community Re-Investment Act requirements imposed upon them by the federal government.

In Cleveland, the Liberty Hill Baptist Church and a group called Neighbors Organized for Action in Housing (NOAH) have led the way in economic development. Together they sponsored a project called Church Square, which combines a shopping mall, anchored by a full-service supermarket, a wide variety of restaurants, and many small businesses like Blockbuster Video and an Allstate Insurance office. There is a day-care center, a medical office complex, and a bank branch office. It also includes sixty single-family houses and ninety-six condominium apartments. This combination of services, employment possibilities, and land development took place on land that had once been the site of abandoned buildings and overgrown vacant lots. I was privileged to be present when both President Bill Clinton and Vice President Al Gore came to Church Square to celebrate this partnership between the religious, business, and civic communities that resulted in the reinvigoration of a once-desolate urban area.

The NOAH project has led to other housing developments in the Hough area of Cleveland. These new housing developments are far from being another instance of gentrification, in which the poor are forcibly removed so that the land on which they live can be redeveloped for an upscale market. The lots on which the new housing in Hough is being built have been vacant since the Hough riots in 1965, when the homes and businesses that once stood there were burned. Thus, the economic-development efforts of one local church, partnered with people in the business community and in government, have ushered in a remarkable wave of jobs, housing, needed services, and a greatly expanded tax base, which helps provide additional services for the community.

In addition to Liberty Hill, other churches in Cleveland have managed to erect high-rise apartment complexes, which in turn have created housing, jobs, and economic opportunity in neighborhoods throughout the city. Greater Abyssinia, Mt. Hermon, and Antioch have all sponsored such housing complexes. In the case of Antioch, we partnered with the Cleveland Clinic and University Circle, Inc., to secure a grant from the Department of Housing and Urban Development to erect a 178–unit building for senior citizens.

What is happening in Cleveland is not unique. The same pattern can be seen through the ministries of Abyssinian Baptist Church of New York City, Hartford Memorial Baptist Church of Detroit, and many others. The moral authority of black middle-class churches, coupled with their locations in the heart of America's inner cities, positions them to be ideally suited to spearhead these kinds of economic-development ventures. Here is another instance in which neither the professional skills nor the financial resources need to reside within the congregation, but the church's willingness to initiate partnerships with other persons and groups can result in significant achievements in areas that would otherwise remain impoverished and underserved.

Credit Unions and Financial-Management Seminars

Not a week goes by that I am not confronted by an inner-city family struggling to overcome past credit problems in order to qualify for a mortgage and a first home. Within the membership of the church are bankers, credit analysts, mortgage lenders, financial planners, and other persons who are uniquely positioned, and usually more than willing, to share their expertise with persons in need. In addition to our own members, there is a steady stream of requests from black persons working in the investment and securities industry who are calling the church to offer their services in financial planning and management.

On any given Saturday morning in the churches in our area, twenty neighborhood residents are sitting in the church basement learning financial skills that will have the effect of helping them turn their lives around. The cost to the church is usually little more than a pot of coffee and making a room available, but the long-term benefit is incalculable. People who are experts in their field are directed to a clientele they might not otherwise encounter in order to equip them with knowledge and information they could not afford to purchase at market prices. This is the church as the salt of the earth.

While helping people handle their finances more responsibly is one thing a local church can do, sometimes the problem is how they can access a loan for a car, debt consolidation, or other purposes when they are still suffering with the results of a damaged or never-established credit history. This is where church-sponsored credit unions can be a great resource. While closely regulated by a national agency, credit unions are able to help people who do not qualify for help from any bank.

Church-based credit unions also serve areas where traditional banks are not willing, for whatever the reason, to place a branch office. Far too many people in inner cities are forced to conduct banking-type business at check-cashing offices that often charge exorbitant fees for paying utility bills, cashing checks, and preparing money orders. Once again, double jeopardy is at work. The people with the lowest incomes and the least access to traditional banks are forced to pay more for services that more affluent bank customers often receive for free. Church-sponsored credit unions can help people cultivate the habit of saving and enjoy the privilege of borrowing money at a fair rate of interest.

The largest black-church credit union in Cleveland is Faith Community Credit Union, which is sponsored by Mt. Sinai Baptist Church. They have assets of over $4 million. At Antioch, our credit union has been in operation since 1946 and has assets of almost $3 million. When added together, the black churches that sponsor credit unions in one section of the city of Cleveland have amassed assets of over $10 million, which is being used to help thousands of people meet their obligations and fulfill their dreams.

Members of our church not only save and borrow through the Antioch Community Credit Union, but they also sit on the board of directors, work in the office during the week, and sit on the credit committee. This is another way by which people's professional skills can be directed into meaningful ministries for the church.

Education from Pre-K through Twelfth Grade

In his book *The Education of Blacks in the South, 1860–1935,* James Anderson reminds us that the church was the first setting in which the education of black people in America took place.[2] Not only were church groups involved in sponsoring colleges, as the African Methodist Episcopal Church did with Wilberforce College in Ohio back in 1856,[3] but classes for freed slaves were held in black churches in the months following the end of the Civil War. Promoting education has long been a focus of black churches — one that must continue.

A church can begin to promote education either by sponsoring a federally funded Head Start program or operating a day-care center for working mothers who need reliable child care so they can get off welfare, hold a job, and become self-supporting. Once again, working in partnership with other churches can be an effective approach. In Cleveland, we have two major agencies that sponsor church-based Head Start and / or day-care services, Community Head Start Agency and Ministerial Day Care Associates (MDCA). Antioch hosts one of the fifteen centers managed by MDCA inside black churches.

The church can become involved in what we in Cleveland call our Adopt-A-School program, which involves churches and major businesses in the city literally adopting a neighborhood school and sending its workers and members into the building to help in ways that the building principal determines. Such involvement runs the gamut from helping in the office to being lunchroom aides, classroom tutors, and library assistants. One of our members, a former offensive tackle for the Cleveland Browns, volunteered with the gymnasium programs. There is not an urban school district in the country that could not benefit from this infusion of energetic volunteers.

Part of our involvement with the Charles Orr Elementary School is to sponsor a field trip at the end of the school year for children who are being promoted out of the building and into middle school. We also help plan and host an end-of-the-year reception following commencement services. I have served both as commencement speaker and as an in-service resource person for teachers in the building. Many of our retired members are especially supportive of this program.

Health and Wellness

The inner-city areas in which so many black middle-class churches are located also happen to be among the most medically underserved areas in the country. This is because many of the residents have no medical insurance and are dependent upon remote county hospitals. They may have to sit for hours in the emergency rooms of charity hospitals. They have no access to private physicians, who offer ongoing health care. Most of all, they are largely unfamiliar with the regiment of information concerning behavioral changes that can contribute to long-term wellness. Here is another area where the black middle-class church can play a significant role.

Leading the way in this area in Cleveland is the Olivet Institutional Baptist Church. One of their deacons is also chief of the medical staff at a nearby teaching and research hospital. His presence in both places helped bring about the Otis Moss Jr. Medical Center in the heart of the inner city. This center houses medical offices for physicians who have admitting privileges with the hospital. It also has a special focus on healthy eating habits that can reduce problems that seem especially severe among black people, such as high blood pressure, kidney disease, stroke, obesity, and diabetes.

The new $1 million building in which the center is housed sits as a jewel in the Fairfax community. More importantly, the medical services it provides are a blessing to people without cars, who can now walk a short distance to receive world-class medical care on par with anything available in the most affluent suburb. Not only do physicians who belong to the church provide medical care, but also church members volunteer to help the church accomplish its health-education programs.

At Antioch, we have partnered with another hospital to focus on the problem of HIV/AIDS. This deadly disease, once perceived as being limited to gay white males, is now spreading most rapidly within the African American heterosexual population. Through a combination of anonymous testing through saliva samples, educational workshops on human sexuality that include discussions of all sexually transmitted diseases (STDs), and a center where persons suffering from AIDS can find support, our center works at both preventing the spread of the disease and at comforting those already infected. Chief on our list of concerns is helping people understand the behaviors, all within their control, that can reduce the transmission of the AIDS virus.

Working with HIV/AIDS inside the church is important for several reasons. First, as a centrally located institution in the community, the church is an ideal place to disseminate prevention and treatment information. Second, persons may be more inclined to come in for testing if it can be done within the community, as opposed to going to some more distant location. Third, it is the epitome of naïveté to believe that all of our churches do not have persons whose lives and families have already been affected by AIDS. In responding to this epidemic within the black community, the black church not only reaches *out* to the people in the community in which it is located. It also reaches *in* to its own membership in a significant way.

There are other ways in which churches can be directed in a ministry that has health and wellness at the center. Much education needs to be done within the African American community at all income levels in areas such as becoming organ and bone marrow donors. Black people lead the list in terms of those who need heart and kidney transplants, but we come in last in terms of persons willing to donate organs for transplant purposes. The church can work with local agencies to arrange for such periodic events as Red Cross blood drives, moderately priced flu shots, prostate screenings for men, and mobile mammography units for breast exams for poor women in the community. Our churches are filled with doctors, dentists, podiatrists, nurses of all types, pharmacists, and hospital dieticians. Working together, they can sponsor health screenings that can provide both early detection and important information to people who might otherwise just get sicker and die.

Voter Registration and Education

Much of what is wrong in America's inner cities could be addressed and remedied if the people who reside in those areas could be persuaded to become registered voters who would then regularly participate in the electoral process. This does not mean only voting on Election Day. It means knowing not only the candidates but the special issues and referendums that appear on a regular basis, many of which have a direct effect upon people living in these areas. Issues such as welfare reform, mandatory sentencing for certain criminal offenses, and the passage of a school operating levy or bond issue are ones that can have an immediate and lasting effect upon life in urban America. The same can be said about such controversial issues as the use of public funds to construct a facility for a professional sports franchise or the diversion of funds from public schools to underwrite a charter school or support a voucher program. These are issues on which the voices of those in the inner city must be heard. The churches in those areas can facilitate this entire process.

People in these areas need to know that it is probably more important to help select juvenile court judges and the county prosecutor or district attorney than any other office on the ballot. The city will only have one mayor and the ward in which one lives will only have one member on city council. However, democracy reaches deeper into the community than that. Who are the ward leaders? Who is willing to run for the job of precinct committee member? Politics is still organized at the grassroots level. These lessons can and should be learned as people gather in churches to organize for political effectiveness.

One of the main roles of the black church dating back to the Reconstruction era has been in this area of political education and organization.[4] Through candidate forums and town meetings with elected officials in a setting in which all sides of an issue can be aired and clarified, the black middle-class church in the inner city can serve as the center of political activity in its community.

Not only can the church be the setting for a variety of explicit political activities, but it can also be the place where local leadership can be identified and groomed for future public service. A church that is sufficiently engaged with the surrounding community quickly comes to know the persons who are willing and able to articulate and represent the interests of that neighborhood. On occasion, the clergy who serve those churches can, and should, make themselves available to represent the community in a political forum. Indeed, there is a long and distinguished history of black preachers who merged religion and politics in ways that proved to be a great blessing to their churches and the communities in which their churches were located.[5]

Of course, nothing is more important than encouraging inner-city residents to actually register and then get out and vote on Election Day. Here in Cleveland, our black, inner-city wards have seen less than 30 percent voter turnout. For instance, I was involved in a congressional primary campaign in May of 1998. There were three black candidates in the race, and it was the most hotly contested and widely discussed political campaign in this area in thirty years. However, only 27 percent of the registered voters went out to the polls that day.

When inner-city residents do not vote, they become the losers. Someone will win the election, and the victor will feel most responsive and accountable to those whose votes put him or her in office. Within the acceptable boundaries of the constitutionally warnings about the separation of church and state, aiding in the area of voter education and voter participation is a critical role that can be played by black middle-class churches.

The church is an important setting for voter registration and education in the community because, as Katherine Tate points out in *From Protest to Politics*, members of black churches are the most politically active and the most regular and consistent voters in the black community.[6] Not only must members of black churches continue their own active role in the political process; they must also help ignite the flame in political activism in the communities where their churches are located. As Charles V. Hamilton points out in *The Black Preacher in America*, the black preacher must lead the way:

> The black lawyer, the black labor leader, the black politician, all these people are growing in number in the black community. But until they develop pervasive, indigenous black organizational structures, they will have to rely heavily on the black preachers for help in reaching and mobilizing the black masses.[7]

Under the leadership of enlightened pastors working within churches that understand and affirm the political role that the black church must play, here is another way in which black middle-class congregations in the inner city can be the salt of the earth.

I have been greatly informed on this matter of political involvement by theological voices from liberal and conservative points of view. I agree with Robert McAfee Brown, who writes

Any Christian worth his salt knows that in this day and age there is an imperative laid upon him to be politically responsible. When one considers the fateful decisions which lie in the hands of the politicians, and the impact which these decisions will have for good or ill upon the destinies of millions of people, it becomes apparent that in terms of trying to implement the will of God, however fragmentarily, politics can be a means of grace.... Politics has become an arena where the most fastidious Christian must act responsibly and decisively if he is not to be derelict in his duties.[8]

I have been equally informed by the viewpoint of the more conservative theologian Carl F. H. Henry, founder of *Christianity Today*, who writes

Does the church belong in politics?... Since God wills the state as an instrumentality for preserving justice and restraining disorder, the church should urge members to engage in political affairs to their utmost competence and ability, to vote faithfully and intelligently, to engage in the public process at all levels, and to seek and hold public office.

The only caution sounded by Henry is one with which I am in full agreement. He says, "The church is not to use the mechanisms of government to legally impose upon society at large her theological commitments."[9]

It must be noted that in order to comply with IRS tax-exempt regulations, churches can neither raise funds for nor endorse any particular political candidate. Beyond that, churches may be actively engaged in politics.[10]

Civil Rights Advocacy

The black middle-class church can play an invaluable role when its members are willing to engage in advocacy on behalf of the people and problems in the inner-city areas in which their churches are located. In fact, such advocacy was commanded by Jesus: "Inasmuch as ye have done it unto one of the least of these..." (Matthew 25:40, KJV). In most black middle-class churches, there is a considerable overlap between membership in the church and in such groups as the NAACP, the National Urban League, Women Speak Out for Peace and Justice, SANE/FREEZE, and other advocacy groups determined to impact American social policies and practices. Such dual membership can be of great advantage.

The church, whether through the pastor or other lay members, also needs to be attentive to instances of police brutality, which tend to be common occurrences in inner-city neighborhoods. Further, the church can be a watchdog that makes sure city services are provided as efficiently in the inner-city areas where they worship as they are in the outlying neighborhoods and suburbs where those members live. In addition, the church may be the only institution able to prevent the Martin Luther King Jr. federal holiday from becoming another excuse for buying a sofa or a car, going to the mall to hang out, or just staying in bed. By showing films, providing guest speakers, and having members of the church tell their story of how they actually participated in some of the campaigns of the civil rights movement, the church can help keep alive a part of black history that we cannot allow to be forgotten or trivialized.

However, the most important thing is for the black middle-class church to demonstrate compassion, first through its own outreach ministries. That being done, the church must also be willing to challenge the agencies of government and the various nonprofit groups in the community to respond to the sometimes desperate needs that exist within the inner cities. These can include such basics as affordable and reliable public transportation, safe and convenient shopping areas for food and other items, and an increased police presence in certain high-crime areas, which will result in a greater sense of safety on the streets and in the parks. All of these activities are overseen by city, county, or state boards. When church members seek either to sit on those boards or to appear before them on behalf of the communities in which their churches are located, they are fulfilling the commandment from Jesus to be salt in the earth. They are also showing their willingness to be careful about the needs of "the least of these."

Traditional Spiritual Programs Open and Available to the Community

Despite all of these areas in which black middle-class churches can be involved as they seek to be the salt of the earth, we must never forget that we are, first and foremost, a community of faith. We establish credit unions, host health fairs, initiate housing programs, and engage in political and civil rights activities, but all of that is what we do in addition to our primary task of preaching and bearing witness to the gospel of Jesus Christ! And we must be sure that we send out every possible signal that the community is as welcome to join us in worship in the sanctuary as they are to gather for a free meal or an AA meeting in the fellowship hall.

The sense of welcome can begin when fliers inviting people in the neighborhood to attend church services are carried to their door, placed in the lobby of their building, or handed out in local stores and businesses. At Antioch, our young people's fellowship does this two or three times a year. Church members can also be present when the social-service programs hosted by the church are in session. That can be an occasion to invite those persons to return for worship, Bible study, or some special musical program.

The most important thing the church has to offer its surrounding community is not its building or its social programs. Our most important offering is the gospel. We tell ourselves each Sunday that our lives will not be complete without receiving Jesus Christ as Savior and Lord. We must be willing to say that same thing to people who may be coming to us only for a hot meal or a cool place to rest. We tell ourselves that "you must be born again" (John 3:7). We must be sure that we are saying that same thing to the people living in the vicinity of our churches.

Having invited neighborhood residents to attend our worship services, we must be careful not to make them feel unwanted or unwelcome because they do not wear the fashionable clothing that so many members of our churches think is absolutely essential. We must be careful to greet them warmly. We must embody the spirit of community without class distinctions that was held up by Paul in Galatians 3:28, where he says, "In Christ there is neither male nor female, neither slave nor free, neither Jew nor Gentile. For you are all one in Christ Jesus" (RSV).

Disciplines for Discipleship
John 8:28–31

N JOHN 8:31, JESUS INTRODUCES A PHRASE THAT IS ABSO-
lutely essential for anyone who wants to be a mature Christian dis-
ciple. He says, "If you continue in my word you shall be my disciple."
The phrasing is so subtle, we could almost read past it and not fully realize
what Jesus is trying to tell us. He is speaking at that point to a group of
Jews who already believe in him; they already acknowledge that he is the
Messiah. But there is something that he wants them to understand clearly.
In those days, to be a faithful Jew was a simple thing. You were born of a
Jewish mother. You were circumcised by a Jewish priest. You obeyed the
Jewish laws as brought by Moses. The question they had for Jesus was,
What did it mean to be his disciple?

That is the question that I want to raise here today. What does it mean,
what does it look like for us to be the disciples of Jesus? In verse 31, Jesus
gives the answer. It does not matter who your parents were. Genealogy is
not important. It does not matter whether or not you have been circumcised.
The only thing required to be a disciple of Jesus is that you continue in his
word; that is to say, every day of your life, for as long as you live, you make a
concerted and determined effort to follow the teachings and the personal
example of Jesus Christ. Discipleship requires daily disciplines.

Let us approach this as if we were trying to lose weight and get our
physical bodies into shape. Far too many people act as if all they need
to do is eat a salad once a week or order a diet soda with their high-fat
and high-calorie meal. Too many people are trying to get in shape by doing
something once a week, maybe even less frequently than that. If you want
to lose weight, you have to work at that every day. You have to exercise discipline on a daily basis. You have to combine exercise and careful diet on
a regular basis. Nobody loses weight by giving up chocolate cake today
but having cheesecake tomorrow. Some things must be done as a matter
of daily discipline.

Jesus tells his followers, then and now, that discipleship requires discipline. It is not enough to attend church once a week, though that is an
important part of being a disciple. Feeding your soul once a week will result in spiritual malnutrition just as surely as feeding your body once a week

---

The author delivered this sermon at Antioch Baptist Church on November 8, 1998. It is
reprinted by permission of *Pulpit Digest;* slight editorial revisions have been made by
Judson Press.

will result in physical malnutrition. Some things must be done every day. Some things must be engaged in on an ongoing basis. Some things must become the *disciplines of discipleship.*

Some months ago in the Wednesday-night Bible class, I shared six spiritual disciplines that I picked up from Haddon Robinson, one of the great preachers of our time. I want to share them with you today. It is my belief that by following these six simple steps on a daily basis, you will be able to do what Jesus commands of us in John 8 – to continue in his word. Let me list all six steps first, and then we will discuss each one in turn. They are

1. live simply
2. love generously
3. serve faithfully
4. speak truthfully
5. pray daily
6. leave everything else to God

Let me start with the first discipline, which is to live simply. Stated another way, this means that we should not spend so much time buying and spending, shopping and consuming. Some people live modest lives without becoming overindulgent or obsessive. Other people are extravagant to a fault. They wake up worrying about to wear. They are always spending more and more on themselves, their home, their wardrobe, their car, their hair and nails. They never have enough. Whatever they earn, they want more. Whatever someone else has, they want to have it as well. They spend until their cash money is gone. They use credit cards until they have reached their credit limit. They put on layaway things they cannot afford to take home today.

There are two problems with this approach to living. One is that many people get themselves into financial trouble, piling up bills they cannot pay to buy things they really do not need. I heard a report on National Public Radio last week that said the average American spends every dime he or she earns each month. While people in other nations around the world are saving 6 to 16 percent of their annual income, most Americans spend all they have. The report also said that the consumer debt index is at an all-time high, which means that after we spend every dime we have, we keep shopping with credit. But since we have spent all of our money, we do not have enough left to pay off our credit cards, so we get killed with 18 to 21 percent annual interest on the amount we owe. Most people will remain in consumer debt for the rest of their lives. If only we could learn to live simply.

This other problem with living beyond our means is the negative effect it has on our second spiritual principle. It is difficult to "love generously" if you consume all of your financial resources by living lavishly. When I speak about loving generously, I am speaking in light of the teachings found in 1 John 3:18, which says, "Little children, let us not love in word…but in deed and in truth" (KJV). For the writer of 1 John, love is not a word that is spoken. It is not a verbal statement. Telling somebody that you love him or her does not mean much if your words are not followed by some actions that put your love into practice. We do not show our love for the people in Honduras and Nicaragua whose lives were devastated by Hurricane Mitch simply by telling them that we love them. Out of our material resources, we need to show them our love in action. We should love generously.

One of my favorite movies is *My Fair Lady*, a movie based upon the novel *Pygmalion* by George Bernard Shaw. It is the story of a girl named Eliza Doolittle, who sells flowers in the streets of London until she runs into a speech teacher named Henry Higgins, who attempts to improve her speech and pass her off as a woman of nobility. At one point in the movie, a young man is attempting to tell Eliza how much he loves her, but she quickly responds to him by saying, "Don't talk of love, show me."

That is what 1 John means by not loving in word but in deed and truth. That is the meaning of the second principle of loving generously. The time will come in the lives of every disciple of Jesus when we will be faced with a tough choice. Will we spend our money on ourselves for something we may not really need or direct those funds to people who face great and urgent needs and who have no place to turn except to us? Loving generously means that we are able to prefer others above ourselves. We cannot just say that we love our neighbor but must actually show that love in tangible ways. And remember that we are talking about daily disciplines. These are not actions that we are expected to do only once in our lives. This is a discipline that Christ wants to see as a part of our daily lives. That is what he means by "continuing in [his] word."

The third principle is serving faithfully. At this point, the issue is doing the very best job you can do on any task that is assigned to you and working hard at it every single time. Almost anybody is capable of giving a maximum effort once on any given project. Almost everybody knows what it is to have gone above and beyond the call of duty on one occasion. However, what this third principle calls for is remaining as faithful tomorrow as you were today, or on any given day in the past. To be faithful means to be consistent. To serve faithfully means that God can count on us on a daily basis.

Terrible things can happen when people who should be faithful every day decide to relax just once. If an airline pilot does not serve faithfully every time, hundreds of lives can be lost. If a surgeon does not serve faithfully every time, the patient may die. If the person who cooks our food does not serve faithfully, people can become sick with food poisoning. If the entertainer we pay money to see does not serve faithfully, we will complain and ask for a refund.

I enjoyed watching the made-for-TV movie about the Temptations, the Motown singing group, which was on last week. I sang along all the way through Sunday and Monday night as the public and private lives of those young men were examined. I grew up singing those songs. I knew every word of the lyrics. I grew up watching the Temptations, and I knew every dance move they made. I cannot tell you how many times I have seen them appear live in concert. I can tell you this, however. No matter how many times they have sung "My Girl" in the past, everybody in the audience each night expects them to sing it with all the passion and polish they possessed when that song was first recorded in 1965. We expect them to serve faithfully. Should God have to expect anything less from us than we expect from those who fly us through the air or treat our medical conditions or prepare our meals or entertain us by singing our favorite songs? I think not! We need to make it our intention to serve God faithfully on a daily basis. This is one of the disciplines of discipleship.

The fourth principle is speaking truthfully. Life is much easier to live when you and I always tell the truth. Then we never have to figure out what the last lie was that we told so that we can retell it in exactly the same way. In a court of law, you place your hand on a Bible, and you "swear to tell the truth, the whole truth, and nothing but the truth, so help you God." If you lie after taking that oath, you are guilty of perjury, or lying under oath. That is one of the charges that surround the talk of impeaching President Clinton.

Jesus says that we should not need that much prompting to tell the truth: "Let your yea be yea, and let your nay be nay" (James 5:12, KJV). Just tell the truth. The risk of being known as a liar is great. Like the boy in the fable who kept crying wolf when there was no wolf in sight, people will not believe you when you finally do decide to tell the truth. This is a sound and solid principle. It does not need much explanation. Just be honest. Just speak truthfully, and do it every day of your life.

The fifth principle is praying daily. I need this reminder because I sometimes allow my life to become so busy with things that I believe to be important that I leave very little time for this simple, but necessary, spiritual practice. Pray daily. This can be an actual time of conversing with God, allowing adequate time for you to talk to God and without rushing on, leaving some time for a quiet moment when God might be able to talk with you. Prayer is not just what we do when we gather on Sunday or at the prayer meeting on Wednesday night. Prayer is what every believer can and should do all through the day.

Ruth Rucker told a story during our fall revival about an older woman, whom she knew when she was growing up, who used to say that she "prayed all through the day." That seemed strange to Mrs. Rucker when she was a younger woman. However, she reported to us that now she also finds herself praying all through the day. Prayer is not what we do only before we partake of a meal, although many people do not pray even then. Prayer is how we stay in touch with God without the need for a congregation, a preacher, a Bible, or a melodious choir. It is the creature's reaching out and up for the Creator. It is the windswept soul in search of a resting place in the midst of this sinful world. Pray daily.

I do not think I have ever felt worse about my spiritual disciplines than I did during a trip to Senegal, West Africa, a few years ago. It was a combination study / sightseeing tour. Senegal is a 95 percent Islamic nation, and our tour guide and bus driver were devout Muslims. I remember one afternoon during a busy tour schedule that both the driver and the tour guide left the group, pulled off their socks and shoes, unrolled prayer mats, and began one of the five regimens of prayer that devout Muslims engage in every day. What a sight. Here was a busload of Christians and Jews anxious to continue their sightseeing. And off in the distance were two Muslims who had stopped what they were doing to engage in the discipline of prayer.

I suddenly felt filled with shame. Here I was – a Christian clergyman – angry with these two men who, I said, were wasting my time. In fact, it was I who was wasting time, rushing around all day and not leaving enough time for prayer. If we are to continue in the example of Jesus, we must make prayer as much a part of our lives as he made it a part of his. Pray daily.

The final principle may be the most important and the most difficult – leaving the rest to God. This principle tries to suggest that there comes a time when life is out of our hands and beyond our direct control. We will have done everything that we possibly can, and still something remains beyond our reach. Loved ones are suddenly thrown into a cycle of sickness. How will they make it? How will you make it without them? Some things we have to leave to God. We raise our children with love and care. Then we send them off to a college campus, knowing full well that they will be exposed to people and practices that can have lasting, negative consequences upon their young lives. But we cannot watch over them every moment. We do not know where they are every second. They are beyond our sight, our reach, our call. But we do have recourse. We can leave the rest to God.

I remember last summer that our son, Aaron, was part of an international wrestling team that went to Kazakhstan, Kyrgystan, and Turkey. For two weeks he was in a country whose name I could barely pronounce, whose spot on the map I had to struggle to find, and whose environment was a throwback to the nineteenth century. They had no telephone system in Kazakhstan, so he could not call us and we could not contact him. Our only son was on the other side of the earth, and as much as we loved him, there was no way for us to make contact.

However, our comfort came in the knowledge that what we could not do, we knew somebody else who could. Where we could not be, we knew somebody else who could. We reminded ourselves that when God created the heavens and the earth, he created the land now called Kazakhstan. He knew where it was. He knew where Aaron was. Peggy and I said our prayers, and then we left the rest to God. Two weeks later our son returned home, and all we could say was, "Thank you, Lord, for doing what we could not do." It may be hard sometimes, but there are those moments when we simply have to realize that the problem or need that confronts us exceeds our resources. That's when it is time to exercise this sixth and final principle and leave the rest to God.

That is what Jesus had to do in Gethsemene when he cried out, "Not my will, but thine be done" (Luke 22:42, KJV). That is what Jesus had to do on the cross when he cried out, "Father, into thy hands I commend my spirit!" (Luke 23:46, KJV). And that is what we have to be wise enough to do as well.

Chapter 5

Competing for the Loyalty of the Black Middle Class

You shall have no other gods before me!

—*Exodus 20:3*

MY FIRST SUNDAY AS THE PASTOR OF ANTIOCH BAPTIST Church in Cleveland was especially memorable because a woman who came through the receiving line at the end of morning worship said something that sticks in my mind to this day. "I will never be in church on third Sundays," she said. When I asked her what was so special about every third Sunday, she responded, "That's the day my sorority meets." I told her how surprised I was to learn of a sorority that met on Sunday mornings at the same time that so many of its members might otherwise be in church. It was then that she assured me that the meeting did not start until 3:00 P.M. However, she remained home on every third Sunday morning so she could "get ready" for her sorority meeting.

Social Clubs and Secret Societies

One of the most interesting and disturbing aspects of ministry in black middle-class churches is how many purely social activities and organizations there are that seem to be equally, if not more, important than any of the activities taking place at or sponsored by the church. I have seen this occur in every setting where I have served over the last twenty-five years, urban and suburban, East Coast and Midwest. It has never ceased to amaze me that members of the black middle class invest as much time and money as they do in these social circles. It often seems to border on devotion.

Those who do ministry with the black middle class must understand that these social activities will often directly conflict with church activities both on Sunday morning and during the week. They will also compete for the same financial commitment that the church would like to secure from its members. Many members of the black middle class will not even join the church because their involvement in these social activities becomes an alternative to involvement in a community of faith.

It is useful to identify the kinds of activities that fit into this category. In some churches, it is groups like the various Masonic and Eastern Star orders, including the Shriners and the Daughters of Isis. The Improved Benevolent Protective Order of the Elks also fits into this group. In other churches, the chief competition comes from the eight college fraternities and sororities. The fraternities are Alpha Phi Alpha, Kappa Alpha Psi, Omega Psi Phi, and Phi Beta Sigma. The sororities are Alpha Kappa Alpha, Delta Sigma Theta, Sigma Gamma Rho, and Zeta Phi Beta. In addition to these, there is a somewhat more exclusive fraternity called Sigma Pi Phi, also known as the Boulé. There is also a professional women's sorority called Eta Phi Beta. Several other groups are designed primarily for black women. Among them are the National Council of Negro Women, the Negro Women's Business and Professional Clubs, and the Links. Two groups are designed to bring together the children of the black middle class: (1) Jack and Jill and (2) Tots and Teens. Added to these are a virtually unlimited array of clubs and groups organized around such activities as professional affiliations, playing cards, dancing, bowling, golfing, investing, traveling, eating, and political organizing. I have never encountered a black middle-class congregation that was not affected by the influence of one or more of these social groups and activities.

Black "Society" as a Response to White Racism

I am not suggesting that these organizations and activities play an unimportant role within the black community. My family and I have been actively involved with many of these groups and activities for most of our lives. It is important to note that most of the groups I have mentioned came into existence in response to America's historic problem of racism. Black people formed these groups, as they formed their churches, because they were denied membership in the white churches, fraternal orders, and social clubs.

Consider the following history. Sigma Pi Phi, organized in 1904, is a direct continuation of the idea of a "talented tenth" as espoused by no less a figure in black history than W. E. B. Du Bois.[1] He was attempting to uplift the race in the face of the vicious racism that black people confronted at the turn of the twentieth century. Those years were so bleak and hostile that the black novelist Charles Chesnutt referred to them as "the nadir or, darkest period, in history for black people in America."[2]

The involvement of black people with the Masonic order dates back to Prince Hall, who organized the first black Masonic lodge in Boston in 1787. He had been initiated in 1775 into Masonry by a British lodge because no white American Masonic lodge would accept black members.[3] I remember my own father explaining to me that he was a member of the *Improved* Benevolent Protective Order of the Elks of the World (IBPOEW), which was organized in 1898. The improvement was that the IBPOEW afforded black people the chance to join the Elks because they were still excluded from the all-white BPOEW. That was as recently as the 1960s.

These same dynamics of racial segregation led Mary McLeod Bethune to organize the National Council of Negro Women in 1935.[4] Racism also resulted in the formation of the National Association of Colored Women by Mary Church Terrell and Ida B. Wells Barnett in 1896.[5] All of the college fraternities and sororities were formed between 1909 and 1945, under the same climate of racial exclusion. So too were the two major civil rights groups: the National Association for the Advancement of Colored People (NAACP) in 1908 and the National Urban League in 1910. The same story of responding to America's history of exclusion and discrimination based solely upon race lies at the heart of why so many professional groups exist that are largely in service to the black middle class. The National Medical Association (1895), the National Dental Association (1913), and the National Bar Association (1925) came into existence because of the policies of racial segregation practiced by whites in these professions.[6]

In each of the above-mentioned organizations, black people wanted to engage in the same activities as their white counterparts. Prevented from doing so on a racially integrated basis, the black middle class organized their own world of professional organizations, secret societies, and social clubs and activities. An excellent discussion of the importance of these social clubs and activities within the black middle class is found in *Black Metropolis* by St. Clair Drake and Horace Clayton.[7] This is an important and honored part of the history of black Americans as we attempted to survive the indignities of racial prejudice and discrimination with dignity and self-respect. Until very recently, the importance of these groups could probably be understood only in relationship to the practice of racial exclusion that had long infected American society.

Social Activities as an Alternative to Church Involvement

The problem discussed in this chapter — competing for the loyalty of the black middle class — has nothing to do with the existence, importance, or mission of the above-named groups. The problem arises when members of the black middle class begin to lose a proper balance between social activities, their spiritual commitments in the church, and the need to assume some responsibility for those persons still confined to the inner cities who need the very help and expertise possessed in abundance by the black middle class. The problem comes when social activities cease to be occasional and temporary diversions and are allowed to become the primary focus in life. The onus of responsibility does not reside with the groups who plan their schedule of activities. It resides with members of those groups who are also members of the church, who must place themselves under the weight of the words of Joshua 24:15: "Choose this day whom you will serve."

A preoccupation with social life was the basis for much of the harsh criticism leveled at the black middle class by E. Franklin Frazier in his 1957 book *The Black Bourgeoisie*. Among the charges made by Frazier is his observation that this preoccupation with social life was a matter of "status without substance."[8] He even talks about black middle-class people who leave the church as soon as they gain some affluence, turning instead to a variety of social activities, with many placing gambling and various sporting events at the very center of their lives.[9]

Frazier ridicules "Negro society" and the regular coverage it receives in such magazines as *Jet* and *Ebony*, which are geared primarily to the black middle class. It is, says Frazier, all about status: "The activities of 'society' serve to differentiate the black bourgeoisie from the masses of poorer Negroes, and at the same time compensate for the exclusion of the black bourgeoisie from the larger white community."[10] Frazier refers to all of this as a life of "make believe."[11]

How ironic that in a quest for social status that hopefully will lift them above other blacks and on par with whites, the black middle class often views even church membership as a social statement. In every major city, there are certain churches where upwardly mobile black people are directed. These churches run the risk of not being the place where you go to meet God but more the place where one goes to meet and be seen by one's peers. Pastors and lay leaders of black middle-class churches must be on guard not only against the groups with whom they compete for the time and loyalty of their congregants. They must also be on guard that their own middle-class churches do not slip into this "status over substance" syndrome and become nothing more than another branch of "black society."

Frazier's critique of the black middle class of the 1950s has been answered by an even harsher analysis from Cornel West. Writing in *Race Matters* in 1993, West observes that the black middle class has increased fivefold in numerical size since the days of Frazier, but he continues:

> Yet this leap in quantity has not been accompanied by a leap in quality. The present-day black middle class is not simply different than its predecessors — it is more deficient and, to put it strongly, more decadent. . . .
> Like any American group achieving contemporary middle-class station for the first time, black entrée into the culture of consumption made status an obsession and addiction to stimulation a way of life.[12]

This observation by West must be taken seriously because it points to one of the primary reasons black middle-class churches cannot accomplish the ministry objectives discussed in chapter 4. People who are preoccupied with social status, the culture of consumption, and the constant pursuit of a new, or a next, thrill are unlikely candidates for accomplishing the kind of work that must take place in the neighborhoods where black middle-class churches are located.

Ministry Interventions in the Battle between Christ and Culture. One of the most important ministries that can be offered to the black middle class would involve regular reminders through sermons, Bible studies, and counseling sessions that the pursuit of social status and the addiction to stimulation are antithetical to the very essence of the Christian faith. Membership in and involvement with these groups are a valued part of life for many in the black middle class. Great care must be exercised, however, so that social activities do not become coequal with or perhaps even an alternative to an active involvement in the ministries of the church.

I have seen this happen on more than one occasion. I have seen men more interested in committing to memory the rituals and procedures of their Masonic lodge than they are in learning or studying the Bible as part of a church-sponsored study program. I have seen women whose church attendance is sporadic, at best, but who would not consider missing a meeting, a luncheon, or a fashion show sponsored by their sorority. I have seen teenagers, with the knowledge and consent of their parents, regularly miss their church activities so they could share in the monthly activities of Jack and Jill. This is an especially dangerous practice because the parents are passing on to their children the idea that parties, cookouts, and trips to an amusement park, scheduled at the same time as Sunday morning worship, are good reasons to skip church on a regular basis.

In raising this issue, I am not suggesting that church membership should be so all-consuming that it neither leaves time for nor tolerates any involvement with social groups or activities. There are some black church groups that do hold to this position. Many of the socially conservative congregations, especially within Holiness and Pentecostal denominations, would encourage their members not to be involved in such activities as fraternities and sororities, Masons and Elks, and especially clubs that involve card playing and dancing. But I am not suggesting that the church should demand that its members have no activities or allegiances beyond the congregation. I am suggesting, however, that black middle-class churches must challenge their members to strike a proper balance between social activities and church involvement.

The God of Heaven versus the Gods of the Earth. What are the gods of the earth that challenge the God of heaven? There are several biblical passages that could be used to assist in answering this question. The most important, however, is found in the first commandment. In relation to social clubs and activities, it is not an overstatement to say, "You shall have no other gods before me" (Exodus 20:3). When lay leaders of a congregation do not attend midweek services because they cannot or will not adjust their bowling schedule, God is being replaced by "a god." When church-school teachers take off from their duties for most of the Sundays between May and October because they must be on the golf course, God is being replaced by "a god."

The issue of time points to another concern. While many members of middle-class churches will be quite faithful in their attendance at Sunday morning worship services, they cannot be counted on for any involvement at any other time during the week. That is, they give God two hours a week, from 11 A.M. to 1 P.M. on Sunday. However, they have no time for Sunday school, midweek services, participation in a church auxiliary, or active involvement in any ministry programs because the rest of their time is spent engaging in a myriad of these social activities. Thus, some members of black middle-class churches will worship God during a closely monitored two-hour block of time on a weekly basis. Others are really more committed to their social lives than they are to their spiritual formation. These members will be in church as long as it does not conflict with a lodge meeting, a fraternity boat ride, a card party, a cookout, or a group outing for brunch. This is a God-versus-gods issue.

I say again, the church need not expect and should not demand that its members totally avoid these activities. There are occasions when the most devout church member may want to miss a church event in order to share in some special activity sponsored by a social group. However, there is room for concern when so many members of middle-class churches do not simply miss church on some rare occasion but are constantly away from church, both on Sundays and during the week. And the reason is clear — they would rather go to a party than go to a prayer meeting.

There is a line in the 1935 film *The Green Pastures* in which Noah says to God, "People around here don't do much church-going. They mostly use Sunday to get over what they did all night on Saturday." Frequently, this is the case in today's black churches. It is at this point that pastors and lay leaders have to raise the first commandment and challenge the members in question to consider what it means to say, "You shall have no other gods before me." When church members are never willing to forgo a social activity out of devotion to the worship and ministry life of their congregation, it is safe to say that God has been replaced by "a god."

The issues addressed by the first commandment are not limited to actual deities that are worshiped in formal ways. What is at stake is anything or anyone that replaces or challenges God as the object of ultimate devotion, loyalty, or trust. In the language of the theologian Paul Tillich, social activities may be of concern to us; they simply should not be of "ultimate concern."[13] Men and women should not become overly attracted to objects and activities, like the idols described in Isaiah 46 and Acts 17, that do not have the ultimate power to offer salvation. Care must be taken not to allow life to revolve around handshakes, passwords, and secret rituals at the expense of giving up or even minimizing our relationship with God. This is the message that must be communicated to the black middle class in general and within the churches of the black middle class in particular.

The Black Middle Class and the Pursuit of Prosperity

Social clubs and their endless stream of activities are not the only things that compete for the loyalty and devotion of the members of black middle-class churches. Pastors and lay leaders of these churches must never underestimate the power and appeal of the American dream and the willingness of people to work to enjoy as much of that dream as possible. The pursuit of that dream often means working on Sundays and leaving little or no time for church involvement.

As shocked as I have been by the number of people who will gladly abandon the church to attend some social event, I have been equally concerned about the number of people who will abandon the church at the prospect of earning some extra money. At any given time in a black middle-class church, members of the congregation will simply be unavailable for long periods of time. Sometimes this is because of a special assignment they must finish either to keep their jobs or earn a promotion. Frequently, however, people regularly forgo church involvement because making money is more important to them. What should the pastor and the lay leaders say and do when the only reason people are missing church is that they have fallen prey to "the love of money" (1 Timothy 6:10)? As Paul says in that same passage, "While some coveted after, they have erred from the faith, and pierced themselves through with many sorrows" (KJV).

The Black Middle Class and Memories of Poverty

The pursuit of prosperity and the American dream is an especially delicate issue with the black middle class. Many of them are the first generation in their families to enjoy any measure of prosperity. They may have grown up, as I did, in very limited economic circumstances. Now they are enjoying all the things they could not afford when they were younger. I can remember never having to wonder what to wear to school the next day because I only had one outfit to put on. I can remember my mother instructing me to take off my Sunday clothes as soon as we got home from church because she could not afford to replace any of it.

My family never owned its own home. When my father abandoned us, I was ten years old. From that time on, we never owned a car. I will never forget standing on the street corners of Chicago in subzero weather waiting for public transportation to take us wherever we had to go. My memories of growing up have helped me understand those persons who, like Scarlett O'Hara in *Gone with the Wind*, have vowed to themselves "never to be hungry again." Most of the time, my circumstances did not seem that dire, largely because most of my closest friends lived at about the same level. But now and then I would be invited to the home of a friend who lived in another part of town, and the contrast between that world and my own would be startling.

Once, when I was about fourteen, our youth group was invited to spend the weekend with a youth group from a white church in our denomination in one of the suburban areas west of Chicago. After the activities at their church, each of us went home with one of those white youngsters for the evening. I went to a house that was the most magnificent thing I had ever seen. I could barely sleep, for looking at all the luxury around me. I will never forget returning home two days later to the inner city of Chicago, to a cramped basement apartment with a ceiling so low I could touch it without even extending my arms halfway above my head. I sat on the sofa in the living room, which at night turned into my bedroom when the sofa pulled out into a bed, and I literally sobbed because the life I had lived for the past two days seemed out of my reach. But I was determined to achieve it someday.

In saying this, I commend my mother for working as hard as she did to hold our family together after my father left us. I do not know if life would have been any better for my brother and me if my father had stayed, but I am sure that it would not have been better for my mother. As it was, she suffered more than her sons did. She lost a husband, a comfortable and spacious apartment in an affluent section of Chicago, convenient access to shopping, and many of her so-called friends, who turned away from her because they thought she would set her sights on their husbands and boyfriends. All of this happened, I am convinced, because my father loved the Improved Benevolent Protective Order of the Elks of the World more than he loved his wife and children.

My story could be matched by almost every member of the current black middle class, though theirs may not always be an experience of urban poverty or the consequences of abandonment and divorce. For my wife, who grew up in northeast Georgia, it was not so much poverty as entrenched racial segregation and the resulting lack of opportunity that kept her ceilings low and her hope dimmed. For others, it was the death of industrial America, the closing of factories, and the loss of good-paying jobs with medical and retirement benefits, exported to Third World countries where workers would be content to earn in a week what Americans once earned in a day.

Whatever the causes, most of us resolved to live a more comfortable life when we became adults because we were scarred by the memories of scarcity, deprivation, and struggle during the years when we were growing up. Our parents' generation had lived through the Great Depression and through the sacrifices necessitated by World War II. For them, poverty and deprivation were a relative thing. Nevertheless, for most black baby boomers, growing up with no concept of home ownership, no access to mainstream society, and no experience with disposable income caused most of us to decide early on that things would be different for us when we grew up. This might have been less true for whites in our age group. The post–World War II years brought stunning opportunities for economic advancement for whites, especially through the GI Bill. Unfortunately, the end of World War II did not bring about the end of racism, segregation, and lack of opportunity for black Americans. Our struggles would last at least another twenty-five years.

So it is that one generation of black people after another has dreamed of living a better life than the generation that preceded it. Those who had known slavery dreamed mostly of freedom. Those confined to tenant farming and sharecropping dreamed mostly of owning their own land. Those who faced the racial hostility of the South at the turn of the twentieth century dreamed of joining the great migration that saw millions of black Americans move to the industrial cities of the North. Those who quickly discovered that the North was not the Promised Land began to dream of civil rights. Every generation has dreamed of experiencing more of what America has to offer than was made available to their parents and grandparents. Church attendance and related activities, while still important, were not going to be an obstacle to fulfilling that dream.

The continual desire of one generation to move beyond the achievements of its predecessors is in evidence in the pointed exchange between a mother and her son in Lorraine Hansberry's 1959 play *A Raisin in the Sun:*

Mama: Son—how come you talk so much about money?

Walter: Because it is life, Mama.

Mama: Oh—So now it's life. Money is life. Once upon a time freedom was life—now it's money. I guess the world really do change.

Walter: No—it was always money, Mama. We just didn't know about it.

Mama: No...Something has changed. You something new, boy. In my time we was worried about not being lynched and getting to the North if we could and how to stay alive and still have a pinch of dignity too.... Now here come you and Beneatha—talking 'bout things we ain't never even thought about hardly, me and your daddy.... You my children—but how different we done become.[14]

The urgency with which many in the black middle class pursue economic opportunities must be viewed with these dynamics in mind.

I fell into the money cycle immediately following my graduation from high school. I attended a vocational school in Chicago, and when I graduated, I had a job waiting for me with Poole Brothers Printing Co. Not only was I making union scale as a regular wage, but I could earn time and a half if I worked on Saturdays and double time if I worked on Sundays. After having grown up as an active member of a church in Chicago, I worked on Sundays without hesitation because in a choice between God and mammon, I chose the mammon. I was determined never again to face an empty closet or a bare pantry. Had my call to ministry not occurred in the summer of 1966 while I was working in that print shop, I wonder if I would ever have broken out of that cycle. While I may have matured somewhat in this area, there are many in the black middle class who are still in hot pursuit of a better life. This is a major issue for anyone who wants to do ministry among the black middle class.

Choosing between the Good Life and the Abundant Life

This conflict between God and mammon can be approached by challenging the congregation to consider the difference between the good life and the abundant life. The "good life" is what America offers at a price. The "abundant life" is what Jesus Christ offers as a gift. And yet there are many people in the black middle class who are much more interested in the good life. It was the English philosopher John Locke, writing in *The Second Treatise of Civil Government* in 1690, who first envisioned the content of the good life. It was, for him, "the right to preserve his property, that is his life, liberty and estate."[15] Thus, the good life has always been envisioned as the process of acquiring, increasing, and enjoying property of one sort or another.

In American history, property has included everything from land and houses to slaves, ships, cattle, commodities, certificates of deposit, and a wide array of consumer and durable goods. Every newspaper ad, television commercial, and sale announcement that arrives in the mail invites people to enter into the good life. If you do not have the available cash to pay as you go, credit can be arranged. And when credit has been exhausted before the urge to consume has cooled, there are layaway options available. Consider a history of poverty and deprivation coupled with the American culture of consumerism, and it is not difficult to understand why so many people in this country are driven by the pursuit of the good life.

The challenge of the church is to call people to a different vision and a different set of priorities. In Isaiah 55:1–2, the prophet seeks to contrast things that cost much but satisfy little with things that cost nothing but bring great satisfaction:

> Ho, every one who thirsts,
>   come to the waters;
> And he who has no money,
>   come, buy and eat!
> . . . .
> Why do you spend your money for that which is not bread,
>   and your labor for that which does not satisfy? (RSV)

Jesus says in Matthew 6:33, "Seek first the kingdom of God and his righteousness, and all these things shall be added to you" (NKJV). He says in John 10:10, "I am come that you might have life, and that you might have it more abundantly" (KJV). Life, liberty, and estate (property) are not unimportant. They must simply be made secondary, leaving us free to engage in our primary duty, which is to be faithful in our duties as Christians.

Being Fulfilled versus Being Filled Full

What is the difference between the good life of John Locke and the abundant life of Jesus Christ? It can best be understood by contrasting the concepts of being fulfilled and of being filled full. Being filled full is all about acquisition and consumption; fulfillment is all about giving, sharing, and sacrificing for the sake of others. Being filled full is how much we can accumulate for ourselves; being fulfilled is how much we are willing to deny ourselves so that others can be blessed and empowered by our generosity. Being filled full is largely informed by a careful reading of the *Wall Street Journal* and *Business Weekly;* being fulfilled is largely informed by a careful reading of the New Testament.

The abundant life is the heart of the message of Jesus. In Matthew 25, he says that heaven is reserved for those who give of themselves to meet the needs of "the least of these." In Matthew 16:24–26, Jesus says, "If any man would come after me, let him deny himself, and take up his cross, and follow me. . . . For what is a man profited, if he shall gain the whole world, and lose his own soul? Or what shall a man give in exchange for his soul?" (KJV).

In Luke 12, Jesus tells the parable of the rich fool, who lays up for himself the wealth of the world and needs bigger barns in which to store his goods. He even says to himself, "Soul, you have ample goods laid up for many years. Take your ease, eat, drink and be merry" (RSV). That very night the rich man died, and his wealth went to someone else. And in Matthew 6:19–21, Jesus flatly warns us against laying up earthly treasures that moth and rust can consume and that robbers can break in and steal. He then sounds the crucial warning that must be preached to those who are in hot pursuit of the good life — "Where your treasure is, there will your heart be also."

Confronting Obstacles to Effective Ministry

This chapter has focused on two issues that, taken separately or together, have the capacity to prevent most black middle-class churches from attaining the focus and commitment necessary to meet the ministry challenges outlined in chapter 4. The quest for the good life and a preoccupation with social activities and organizations can leave people without the time, energy, or interest needed for the church to make a difference in the world.

The words of Cornel West about the lifestyle of many in the black middle class are true: "The present-day black middle class is not simply different than its predecessors — it is more deficient and, to put it strongly, more decadent."[16] Overinvolvement in social activities and the pursuit of prosperity are two of the primary reasons this is so. But biblical and theological themes can serve to reverse the trend. There is no better place to start than within the numerous affluent, but apathetic, black middle-class churches. Let us preach a gospel message that, in the words of Harry Emerson Fosdick, warns against a church that is "rich in things and poor in soul."[17]

Steps toward Becoming a Whole Person
Mark 6:30–33

I PREACHED MY FIRST SERMON AT THE AGE OF SIXTEEN IN my home church in Chicago. I had just shared the early sense of my call to ministry with the pastor, and he had me preach as a way of seeking further confirmation of what God was doing. I remember that event as if it were yesterday. I preached about the steps that lead to a complete life, based upon Luke 2:52, which says, "And Jesus increased in wisdom and stature, and in favour with God and man" (KJV). I suggested in that sermon (or more appropriately, in that short talk) that Jesus was the man that he was because he grew physically and spiritually, and because he was pleasing to God and popular with other people.

Thirty-four years later, I am still intrigued by the signs of a rich and full life. What are the things we should be doing if we want our lives to reach the full potential that God has intended for each of us? I am aware of the insights that two other great men have offered in this pursuit. Martin Luther King Jr. wrote a famous sermon entitled, "The Measure of a Man," in which he spoke about the *height, depth, breadth*, and *length* to which the human spirit can be stretched. I was reading a short biography of Frederick Douglass just last night. In it, that writer noted that Douglass was driven by a set of deeply held principles, which included hard work, perseverance, thrift, moral convictions, and religious faith. It is interesting to observe that people have long been searching for some way to measure and mark the growth and development of human life.

I want to look at this issue of the steps that lead to becoming a full and complete person. I want to point to five steps that I believe that you and I need to take to protect our physical health, to nourish and nurture our intellect, to lend a helping hand to those in need, to maintain a close relationship with our family, and to sustain a constantly refreshed relationship with God. Let me suggest today that a complete life is based upon the assessment of several areas of our lives, and not just one or two. Using these five criteria — health, head, helping hands, home life, and a heart for God — how healthy and complete is your life?

We need to measure the health of our existence by doing the same thing doctors and nurses do when determining the physical health of our bodies. They do not check just one vital sign and then pronounce that we are

This sermon was delivered by the author at Antioch Baptist Church on April 25, 1999.

healthy or ill based solely upon that one measurement. Rather, they check several areas and make their decision about the state of our physical health based upon what they discover.

Anyone who has had a thorough and comprehensive medical exam lately knows that no one area of your body is examined. You are checked from head to toe and from the inside out. During my last exam I had to fill out an extensive medical-history form. Then I provided samples of various bodily fluids. My blood pressure was taken on both arms, and my pulse was taken in both a resting and an active setting. My weight was then calculated in relation to my height. I was probed and prodded for more than an hour, and then all of that information was considered together to determine the state of my physical health. No doctor would offer an analysis of a patient's physical health by simply considering one set of data. Instead, several areas are reviewed and considered together.

The same thing is true when we look to determine the overall health of our lives as people, as citizens, and as Christians. Do not look at any one thing, but look at several areas and consider them together. That is what these five vital signs of human existence offer us – a method by which each one of us can determine the quality and character of our own lives. If we were to review your physical health – the time you spend nurturing your mind, the hours you spend extending a helping hand to others, the commitment to spending time with your family, and the various things you do to maintain a refreshed and rewarding relationship with God – how would your life look today?

It is all a matter of time management. We need to *make* the time or *take* the time to do those things that make our lives most rewarding. We need to take the time to protect our health. Some people keep themselves so busy that they leave no time to rest, no time to renew their strength. That is where this text comes in. Jesus had sent his disciples out for their first experience in ministry. They had gone out two by two, and it seems that every minute of every day had been filled with activity. When they returned to Jesus at the end of their mission, they began to report what they had done. Immediately the crowds of people began to appear, coming to be healed and to hear the preaching of the gospel. One demanding schedule was being replaced by another, with no time whatsoever in between. That is when Jesus took his disciples away from the crowd for a time of renewal and rest.

As it was for them, so it is for us today. Every now and then, we need to go apart from the crowd so we can be refreshed and renewed, and *that* begins with the need to rest and maintain the health of our bodies. How greatly our ability to serve God is impeded if we work and run ourselves into the ground, lose good health, and are always sick simply because we didn't take the time to remain healthy. I guarantee you; one of you here today is sick because you never took the time to take care of your health. I have told you before about my college roommate who was complaining of numbness in his fingers and toes at the age of twenty. He would not go to the doctor. He was too busy. He had exams to study for, parties to attend, and other things that he believed simply could not wait. However, one Saturday night he suffered a fatal stroke as a result of blood clots. His body had been telling him that something was wrong, but he would not listen, and he never lived to see age twenty-one.

What sense does it make to say that you want to serve in the army of the Lord, but you are too sick or too feeble to function? In the movie *The Ten Commandments*, Moses gives the Hebrew slaves one in every seven days to rest. When he is challenged about that decision, he answers by saying, "The strong make many bricks, the weak make few, and the dead make none." If you want to be a soldier in the army of the Lord, begin by taking care of your health. You cannot do much for God without it.

Then take equally good care of your head. Never stop feeding your intellectual grasp of the faith. To be a Christian is not simply to be involved in the work of ministry. It is also to be engaged in the study of the Word. In this world where our faith is constantly under attack from critics on the one hand and competitive religions on the other, we need to know what the Word of God says. We need to feed and feast upon the Bible. And beyond that, we need to remain aware of the ideas and thoughts spreading through the world that may be dangerous or destructive. Do not be content to have a healthy body, if it is to be accompanied by an empty head.

Yesterday at the annual luncheon for READ (Reading Enrichment for Adult Development), I reminded those in attendance of the story of a great football player named Dexter Manley. He was both an all-American and an all-pro defensive lineman. Since he was such a remarkable athlete, teachers did not notice or did not care that he could read only at a second-grade level. He was a grown man who was a magnificent physical specimen, but he had never taken as much time for his head as he had for his health. When his playing career was over, he had to go back to school and learn how to read so he could have a reasonable, decent life. A strong body coupled with a weak and untrained mind is a bad combination.

How many of our own young people are falling into this very same problem? They spend endless time and money on their exterior appearances, whether that means hairstyles, designer fingernails, famous-label clothing, or trips to gyms and salons. But they cannot pass the state's ninth-grade proficiency exam. They cannot fill out a job application to secure employment. They look good on the outside, but their brains are like an empty wasteland. God wants us to serve him with good health and a good mind. Both of these are important areas to consider when assessing whether or not we are becoming all that God wants each one of us to be in life.

The next area of measurement deals with the degree to which we are ready and willing to lend a helping hand to others who are in need. It does not matter if you are physically fit and intellectually alert, if your sense of human compassion is dull and lifeless. Part of what God looks at is how you and I respond to others in their times of distress. Notice the language in Matthew 25 in the Great Judgment scene. Jesus says, "I was hungry – thirsty – naked – sick – imprisoned." These are conditions in which people can find themselves. The question, however, was not their condition. The question was whether anybody came to their aid. Jesus wants to know, in the face of these conditions, whether you did or did not feed – give drink – visit – care for – clothe. How do you and I measure up in the helping-hand category?

Most of us are willing to help if somebody specifically knocks on our door and requests our assistance, and that is a good thing. But how much sweeter it is when the help comes as a result of our own initiative and not because we had to prompt someone into action. A month ago, as a result of a strong wind, a very long and heavy branch from one of the trees in our backyard fell down. The force of the fall caused several pickets in the fence where it landed to be knocked off. The limb now rested on the telephone and cable lines, which looked as if they might snap at any moment. I called the respective utilities, but nobody came to remove the limb. One day I put on my work gloves and went back there to remove the branch myself. I managed to push the limb off the wires, but it was so long that, no matter on which side of the fence I stood, I could not get a good enough grip on the limb to pull it away. Given how it was situated, with one end in one backyard and the other end reaching over to the next yard, it was too long and too heavy for one person to handle.

Just as I was considering whom I was going to call to come and lend me a helping hand, one of my neighbors showed up with his work gloves on. He never said a word. He did not ask if I needed help. He saw what was happening and simply volunteered. He got in one yard and I got in the other, and together we got that limb over the fence where I could drag it out to the curbside. By the time I came back to thank him for his help, he had already returned home. But his kindness and helpfulness warms my heart to this day.

This is a true and accurate measurement of the fullness of our humanity. Are we willing to help our neighbors and others who pass our way, even when no specific request for that help has been made? That is the meaning of the gospel popularized by Mahalia Jackson song that says:

> If I can help somebody as I pass along,
> If I can cheer somebody with a word or song,
> If I can show somebody he is traveling wrong,
> Then my living will not be in vain.

The fourth area to be considered when looking to see whether or not our lives are as fully developed as God would like them to be is whether we take time for that central social institution, which is the family. The nature of our family relationships may vary. You may not have had both parents in the home. You may have been raised by foster or adoptive parents. You may have been an only child or one of a dozen or more children. But regardless of our histories or our current situations, we should never get so busy in life that we leave no time for our families.

This applies as much to the pastor as it does to the people. In a sense, I have two families, the family of Antioch and the family of McMickle. In my case, both have a fairly equal claim. But I have to be careful that I do not spend so much time with one that I do not leave adequate time for the other. Catholic priests do not have this problem. They take a vow of celibacy that rules out the chance for marriage or fatherhood. They literally marry the church, and they are free to give all of their time in one direction. In the case of Protestant clergy, we have football games, wrestling matches, band concerts, science fairs, birthday parties, PTO meetings, and so much to include in our lives. (And I would not have traded those things for anything in this world.)

What about you and your family? Are you so busy making money, attending social events, being involved in all of the clubs and boards and organizations that you have no time for your family? Are you helping your children grow up or just watching from a distance? As the details of what happened last week in Littleton, Colorado, slip out, it is clear to me that a little more direct parental involvement in the lives of those two young men who were the killers could have made all the difference in the world. Did the parents not know how their children dressed to go to school? Did the parents not know the video games their children played at home? Did the parents not see the guns and bomb-making equipment lying in clear view in their own garage? Now these same parents ask the question, "What went wrong in the lives of our children?" The answer is not very complicated. Children must be raised and trained, not just housed and fed. It would mean very little for me to work hard to keep the Antioch family in good working order, if my own family at home were in chaos and disarray. If you and I get to be too busy to be meaningfully involved with our own families, whatever the makeup of that family might be, we are simply too busy.

Finally, a whole and complete life is one that is regularly nourished and refreshed by a relationship with God and God's people. As the pastor of a middle-class black congregation, I am especially concerned about this area because there is a great danger that, as our economic prosperity increases, our relationship with God and God's people may be allowed to decrease. We may become so caught up with our clubs, fraternal groups, cotillions, cabarets, and cocktail parties, that we allow a serious relationship with God to become only a marginal aspect of our lives. When we lived in a segregated society and suffered under the pressures of poverty, our relationship to the church was much stronger, perhaps because going to church was one of the very few things we were free to do. Most of us did not have cars to wash on Sunday. We did not have golf foursomes that took priority. We did not go to brunch on the Lord's Day. We did not buy into the slogan used in a recent advertisement for the *New York Times*. A black woman is shown sitting at home reading the Sunday edition of that newspaper, and she says, "Sunday is for the *New York Times*."

There was a time when Sunday was for the Lord. There was a time when Sunday was defined by the words of Psalm 122:1, which says, "I was glad when they said unto me, let us go into the house of the LORD" (KJV). The more prosperous we become, the more we have to be attentive to our spiritual health. We are in danger of falling into the same trap that the majority population of this country is already in. The words "In God We Trust" are engraved on our national currency. However, what most people in America really trust is the money, not the motto on that money. We in the black middle class must be careful about our spiritual health.

As Christians we need to be careful about spiritual health because we might make the mistake of trying to substitute church work for real Christian worship and church auxiliaries as an alternative to congregational praise. It is not enough to simply be in the church if you are not also caught up in the spirit. And try as you might, you cannot become all that God wants you to become as a Christian if you isolate yourself from the larger community of faith. Take time to fill your heart with the things of God in the context of the gathered and assembled people of God.

That is also what Jesus was doing with his disciples when he took them aside for a time. They had been involved in the work of the church. They had been feeding the poor, healing the sick, and preaching the Good News to the people. But all of that was what they were giving to others. When did they take the time to nurture and nourish their own souls and spirits? That is what happens to so many good Christians; they are busy meeting the needs of others, but they do not take time to have their own souls refreshed in worship, prayer, praise, and study. This, of course, says nothing about those Christians who are attempting to get to heaven on the installment plan, making an occasional appearance in church once a month or once every other month or once a year or even less. They may get into heaven, but it will be because God is gracious and not because they have been faithful.

Of all the things that make a demand upon your time, please be sure to leave adequate time for your relationship with God and God's people. Leave time for worship and fellowship. Leave time for praise and congregational prayer. Leave time for Sunday morning and Wednesday night. Leave time, not just for the tangible work of missions and service, but for the intangible work of spiritual growth and renewal. And be careful if the pace of your life begins to pick up to such a degree that you find yourself having to miss church for one seemingly good reason or another. If you have to use Sunday morning in order to do your schoolwork or your career work or to pursue your social or civic agenda, dear friends, you are not putting your time to the best possible use. As the songwriter says, it takes "time to be holy." And as the anonymous poet also says:

> I have only just a minute,
> Only sixty seconds in it —
> Forced upon me, can't refuse it,
> Didn't seek it, didn't choose it,
> So it's up to me to use it.
> I must suffer if I lose it,
> Give account if I abuse it,
> Just a tiny little minute,
> But eternity is in it.

With the time that God has given you, take time to do those things that will result in your becoming the complete and responsible human being that God intends for all of us to be. Take time for your health, your head, your helping hand, your home, and your heart. And do not waste time, because how you and I will spend eternity hangs in the balance.

Chapter 6

The Black Middle Class and Responsible Christian Stewardship

And there was a certain beggar named Lazarus, which was laid at his gates, full of sores.

—*Luke 16:20*

T HAS ALWAYS BEEN QUITE CONVENIENT FOR BLACK PEOPLE to read the story of the rich man and Lazarus from the perspective of the victim. Many of us could very easily identify ourselves with the plight and position of Lazarus. For more than two hundred years, our people had sat at the gates of America hoping to consume a few of the crumbs of freedom, opportunity, prosperity, or justice. We could also identify with Lazarus after his death, when he was taken to heaven and rested in the bosom of Abraham. The idea that God would somehow compensate us after death for the indignities and injustices we had suffered in life, as was the case for Lazarus in the parable, is consistent with the "pie in the sky" theology discussed first by Benjamin E. Mays in *The Negro's God As Reflected in His Literature* and later by James Cone in *The Spirituals and the Blues.*[1]

Whenever I have heard this story used in the black church, the objective always seemed to be to comfort the afflicted. However, I have never forgotten a lesson of biblical interpretation offered by my Old Testament professor, James Sanders, at Union Theological Seminary in New York City. He would often warn us that if our reading of a biblical passage left us feeling good about ourselves, we could be sure that we have misinterpreted that text. More often than not, the Bible serves to afflict the comfortable. It serves to prod us away from being content with the status quo. It urges us not primarily to use the text as a basis for judging the faithfulness of others; rather, it challenges us to use the text as the basis for judging our own faithfulness.

James Sanders offered us an additional insight on biblical interpretation. Writing in *Canon and Community*, he observes, "All humans in the Bible, save one, are shown as sinful."[2] He also taught us that the Bible could be read either as a model or a mirror of morality.[3] If it is read as a model, then the reader can say, "I want to be like a certain biblical character," and Bible characters set the standard to which the reader should aspire. However, if the Bible is read as a mirror, then the reader can say, "I am like that biblical character." In this scenario, the Bible reflects human nature in all of its sinful ways. The Bible does not show us who we should become; it shows us who we are. It revolves around Romans 3:23, which says, "All have sinned and fall short of the glory of God."

I have come to read the story in Luke 16 as a mirror. No more can I take comfort in the way in which Lazarus is portrayed, for this text severely afflicts the comfortable members inside black middle-class churches with regard to their stewardship. More particularly, this text should challenge us at the level of our willingness to use our financial resources to help uplift the quality of life for people living in the inner-city areas where our churches are located.

On the whole, the vast majority of members of black middle-class churches have long since ceased to be Lazarus. The parking lots of our churches filled with Lexus, BMW, Mercedes Benz, and Lincoln automobiles are early indicators of that fact. So too are the mink coats, Rolex watches, Mont Blanc pens, Louis Vuitton bags, and the accessories and other articles of clothing that serve as proof of our arrival into the ranks of the middle class. Home ownership, tuition receipts from elite colleges and private schools, savings accounts and investment portfolios, frequent trips to Europe and Africa, and cruises through the Caribbean are the characteristics of today's black middle class. No. The black middle class would have a very difficult time casting itself as Lazarus, full of sores and begging for crumbs.

We are, more appropriately, the owner of the house at whose gates Lazarus is laid. We are much more accurately cast as the rich man clothed in purple and fine linen who ate sumptuously every day. The question in this chapter is whether we can and will walk past Lazarus, lying at our doors, as we come in and out of our churches. Or will we find a way to direct some significant portion of our wealth and resources toward helping Lazarus to be properly fed, housed, and clothed? Will we help the Lazarus community outside our doors break addictions to drugs and alcohol? And will we help Lazarus find the way either to a classroom or a job? Or like the rich man in the parable, will we simply come and go and pay no attention to the needs of the poor of our own race, living in the shadow of our stately church buildings?

How the black middle-class church does or does not use its financial resources to address the needs of the poor and needy who are at our church doors every day carries with it a significant consequence. In the language of Luke 16, this will determine whether we will or will not join the rich man in the flames of hell. Pastors and lay leaders of black middle-class churches must challenge their congregants to see that membership in the church also involves discipleship and stewardship. There are actions we must engage in on behalf of others, and one of those actions involves financial support of the ministries and programs of the church. Members of black middle-class churches must be challenged to increase their financial support of the church as their own personal resources increase. We dare not see our incomes go up dramatically while the level of our stewardship remains frozen.

From Waiting for a Check to Sending One

There is a mental transformation that must take place if the black middle class is to mature in the area of Christian stewardship. First, we must stop thinking about a check as something we receive from others. Second, we must begin to think about a check as something we can reasonably be expected to send to those in need.

Some people in black middle-class churches will undoubtedly have had some history with welfare, disability, social security, child-support programs, and other governmental agencies from which they received a check. They may have had less experience with writing checks to the United Negro College Fund or their own college alma mater, the Sickle Cell Anemia Foundation, the American Red Cross, a local arts institution, a political candidate or cause, a homeless shelter, or public radio and TV. The conscious and visible shift from receiving public funds to underwriting and supporting public agencies and nonprofit programs is a mind shift that those in the black middle class must be encouraged to make.

There is a quick and painless way to determine how far along a person is in that process. Take a look at the canceled checks from the bank at the end of each month. If the majority of the checks, or the majority of the expenditures, goes to credit-card companies, clothing stores, consumer goods, and other things that show people to be investing in themselves, that is one thing. If there are checks in generous amounts made out to the church, other charitable causes, and a variety of community efforts that benefit other people, that sends a very different and a much better message.

Philanthropy need not be thought of as the millions of dollars given by the superrich captains of industry from John D. Rockefeller at the end of the nineteenth century to Bill Gates at the end of the twentieth century. It can and should be thought of as the more modest amounts given by people of middle-class means who simply want to express their concern for those in need and express their gratitude to God for their own blessings of health and prosperity. The black middle-class church needs to help its members take on this new mind-set. Giving habits will not be changed until minds have first been changed. Stewardship with regard to our financial resources must be informed by solid faith principles. Jesus tells us, "For where your treasure is, there will your heart be also" (Matthew 6:21, KJV). There is an inescapable connection between the causes and issues we believe to be important and the level of financial support we are willing to invest in those areas.

Becoming a Tithing Congregation

Two steps can be taken by every congregation to effectively increase the level of economic support for the work of ministry. The first step is to become a tithing congregation. By *tithing*, I do not mean simply that people should be asked to give 10 percent of their income to the church. It is my view that nothing contributes more to the lack of support that so many churches experience than constantly harping on the amount of money members should contribute to the church. Some churches take their tithing program to such an extreme that those members who have not yet committed to give at that level are made to feel like second-class citizens in the church.

All this is not to say that I discourage tithing. To the contrary, I wholeheartedly believe that Christians should tithe 10 percent of their income and have practiced it myself for many years. But I have found that people are more likely to give 10 percent of their income to the church when the church makes the commitment to give 10 percent of its annual revenues to programs and ministries that serve people beyond their congregation. That is to say, tithing should be understood as a two-way flow of funds. Members of the congregation should be challenged to bring into the church 10 percent of their annual income. At the same time, the congregation should agree to contribute 10 percent of its annual operating budget to programs and agencies whose work is consistent with the ministry and the mission of the church and whose efforts are in support of the same people that the church desires to help.

Practicing What We Preach. A tithing church should not be defined only with regard to how much money comes into the church. Of far more importance is the willingness of the church to act on the same faith principles it uses to solicit contributions from its members. We tell them that if they bring their tithes into the storehouse, God will open the windows of heaven and pour out blessings upon them (Malachi 3:10). We challenge our members to believe that if they are generous in their giving to the church, God will provide for their needs.

It is just as important that the congregation act upon that same principle. God can and will bless a generous congregation as easily as a generous donor to that congregation. It may be that many of our churches lack the financial resources they need to retain a competent staff, maintain adequate facilities, and conduct an effective outreach ministry because they devote most of their creativity to fundraising rather than to missions support. Would it not be sinful for a congregation to fail to trust God enough to give 10 percent of its annual income in support of programs and ministries that bless and benefit the lives of persons outside their doors?

Applying "More Blessed to Give Than to Receive" to the Church. As a demonstration of the faith that the church wants to see in its members, the church should commit to being a tithing congregation in terms of the amount of its annual budget it agrees to direct toward its outreach ministries. This commitment must be viewed as being as important as paying the staff, providing for the maintenance and utilities for the church building, purchasing robes and music for the choir, and providing funds for youth ministry, Christian education, and church suppers and other times of congregational fellowship.

This commitment to being a congregation that tithes from its annual budget should be made whether or not the majority'of the members of the congregation are themselves already giving at a 10-percent level. That was our decision at Antioch, and our contributions from the membership have greatly increased. Rather than waiting until the membership was giving at a 10-percent level before the church did the same, we reversed the order. We committed to giving to others 10 percent of our annual budget, and we challenged the membership to follow that example. What we say to our members about their not being able "to beat God's giving" as far as their individual stewardship is concerned, works just as well when directed toward the stewardship commitment of the congregation. God will not only bless a tithing member of the church who gives 10 percent to the church; God will also bless a tithing congregation that donates 10 percent of its annual operating budget to ministries that meet the human needs outside their door.

There is no excuse for the failure of a black middle-class church to tithe. The resources are there in the membership. It is no more appropriate for the church to hold back its funds for personal use than it is for a church member to use that excuse for not tithing to the church. Here is one way the black middle-class church can be a blessing to the community in which it is located.

We condemn white-owned businesses that operate in the inner city, make their profits from black residents, and then fail to reinvest any of their profits in that same inner-city community. How much worse is it when the black church operates on the same model? We gather in the inner city. We erect elaborate churches for ourselves. We sponsor marvelous programs for our members and their friends. When the day is done, we lock the doors, set our burglar alarms, secure our churches behind barbed-wire fences, and return to the suburbs or outlying city neighborhoods, confident that we have pleased God that day. In the meantime, we have not intentionally invited into our churches the people huddled just beyond our buildings. Nor do we intentionally direct any significant portion of our operating funds toward the relief of their needs. There is a very great danger that many black middle-class churches reenact the story of the rich man and Lazarus in Luke 16 on a weekly basis. That trend can be reversed if the church is as committed to tithing 10 percent from its annual budget to missions support as it is in encouraging its members to tithe 10 percent to the church. The words of Jesus, "It is more blessed to give than to receive" (Acts 20:35), which the church uses to encourage members to give generously, are no less true when directed toward the giving patterns of the congregation itself. This commitment to becoming a tithing church is the first step.

Letting the Congregation Designate Mission Funding

The second step to improved stewardship in churches can be achieved when the congregation plays a larger role in determining where the funds designated for mission and program support should be directed. It is unreasonable to expect that people in middle-class churches, many of whom are making major personal and professional financial decisions every day, will increase their financial support for any program that allows them no voice or vote in determining where those funds should be directed. It is just as important for the church to affirm where their funds are being directed as it is for the church to make 10 percent of their funds available for missions and outreach. The question is, how can such a consensus be created? Let me offer one model that can be adapted to the needs and preferences of any congregation.

Achieving Congregational Ownership of the Benevolence Budget. At Antioch, we vote every year on a benevolence budget. The dollar amount is 10 percent of the operating budget. Note that this 10 percent is not taken from the operating budget; it is an additional 10 percent. As pastor, I establish a broad set of categories in which we ought to be supportive. They include support of the work of our denomination. We then support a wide array of civil rights groups, educational and scholarship programs, health and medical research agencies, arts and cultural institutions that specialize in black history and culture, disaster relief both locally and beyond, after-school tutorial programs for neighborhood children, and hunger centers and food pantries.

We also include other direct service groups who work with needy people on a daily basis. This includes groups like the City Mission, which provides meals and clothing for a largely homeless population. Mindful of the number of colleges and universities in the Greater Cleveland area, we support the University Christian Ministries, which support chaplains on local college campuses. We support the United Black Fund, a local version of United Way sponsored by the black community, which funds programs of various types within the inner city. We also partner with other faith-based groups and programs that serve the needs of families in the communities that surround our church.

I propose an initial budget amount. The elected officers of the church review that proposal. They can propose that the categories be cut, that the amounts be adjusted, or that my suggestions stand as presented. They vote to recommend this benevolence budget to the congregation. At a church meeting, the same process is repeated. Categories can be cut, and amounts can be adjusted. This is the part of the process that is most valuable. Here is where the congregation speaks about how and where it wants to direct the funds they have brought to the church. This is where ownership of a 10-percent commitment to congregational support of other programs is accomplished. In the years since we began this process, the only debates we have had involved removing from the list those agencies that did not seem to be accomplishing the work they had taken on. We also debated when and how to add new agencies that could help us maintain a ministry that was relevant to the changing needs of our world.

Every year we leave 15 percent of the benevolence budget undesignated so that we have some flexibility and capability to respond to needs that may arise over the course of the year. We were able to direct $5,000 to relief for the people of Honduras after the hurricane in the summer of 1998 devastated that country, and another $5,000 to relief for the people of Kosovo in 1999.

Reflecting Responsible Christian Stewardship in Other Ways. Supporting people and programs beyond the church doors can also be done in ways that do not involve making financial contributions to the church. There are endless groups needing a variety of supplies that can be provided through the church, by its members, for the benefit of others. Homeless shelters and shelters for battered women and their children always need toiletries, clean sheets and towels, and even furniture.

Black middle-class churches should also seek opportunities to reach a helping hand across the ocean to the nations and people of Africa. Appeals are constantly being made for school supplies of all sorts in mission-sponsored schools across that continent. At Antioch, we probably have enough books, pens and pencils, rulers and calculators, and other such supplies to equip a school in an African country for a year. In fact, in 1998 Antioch did just that for a school in Malawi and another in Zimbabwe. It is amazing how the story of the multiplication of fish and loaves comes alive at this point. Our little becomes so much when we place it in the hands of Jesus, who then directs it toward those who are greatly in need.

A Biblical Mandate
for Responsible Stewardship

In order for a black middle-class congregation to accept the challenge to become a tithing congregation, not just seeking to bring funds in but organized and committed to giving at an equally significant level, a strong biblical rationale must be established. The biblical material that can be used to help make this point is abundant, but there is one text that is particularly appropriate. It involves the words of Jesus, "To whom much is given of them will much be required" (Luke 12:48, RSV).

It can surely be argued that the black middle class is the beneficiary of the efforts of many who have come before them in previous generations. Few, if any of us, are self-made people. Our freedoms were secured by the sacrifices and struggles of earlier generations that opened the doors of political, economic, and educational opportunity that we now enjoy. In many instances, the very church buildings in which we gather to worship were built, paid for, and passed on to us by earlier generations.

Many in the present black middle class are directly indebted to the efforts and results of the civil rights movement. The *Brown v. Board of Education* decision in 1954 opened up educational opportunities long denied to those who came before them. The 1964 Civil Rights Act and the 1965 Voting Rights Act provided protections for the constitutional rights of black people, which had long been denied their forebears. The work of such early political leaders as Congressman Adam Clayton Powell Jr., Mayor Carl Stokes of Cleveland, and Federal Judge Constance Baker Motley blazed the trail that hundreds of black politicians now walk at every level of government.

The quality of life available to present members of the black middle class is nearly unimaginable, possibly unrecognizable, even to their own parents. I earned more at the beginning of my career in 1972 than my mother did at the end of her career in 1980. There are probably such examples in every black middle-class congregation throughout the nation. Those of us who constitute the The black middle class can respond to this shift in historical circumstances in two ways. We can gloat over our personal achievements and simply enjoy the fruits of our labor. Or we can recognize how indebted we are to the efforts of those of earlier generations who labored, sacrificed, and suffered to make a better life for those who came after them. In my own case, the fact that I earned more at the beginning of my career than my mother did at the end of hers is only half the story. The other half, the far more important half, is that the education I received that empowered my career was made possible by the enormous acts of self-denial my mother endured so that my tuition could be paid and my other needs could be met. It is with this personal sense of indebtedness to her, and to her generation of black and white people, that I say these words to the black middle class: "To whom much is given, of them will much be required" (rsv). This is a solid rationale for responsible Christian stewardship!

From Praise and Prosperity to Being My Brother's Keeper

One major theological hurdle must be cleared if Christians of any and all races and classes are to become mature and responsible stewards, sharing their financial resources with others through the ministries of the church. We must move beyond the popular view heard so frequently today that the chief concern that God has for our lives is that we be prosperous. I have heard more than a few sermons in which praising God was the spiritual equivalent of milking a cow. If you go through the right procedures, something good will come your way. So, we are told to worship God so that he will send blessings upon us. We are told that "when the praises go up, the blessings come down."

All of this has the effect of making us, and not God, the center of the worship experience. We do not worship God because of who God is or because of what God has already done for us through the death, burial, and resurrection of Jesus. Under the umbrella of this prosperity gospel, we do not worship so that God may be praised as an end in itself. Instead, we worship so that we will be blessed. God is not being honored; God is being induced. In fact, we are not serving God; God is actually serving us.

This prosperity gospel has been pawned off on the black community by charlatans like Rev. Ike in New York City. It has been satirized in the film *Car Wash*, in which Richard Pryor plays the role of Daddy Rich, pastor of the Church of Divine Economic Spirituality. It can be heard in sermons preached across this country, on radio and cable TV programs.

The problem posed by this understanding of worship is obvious. How do you persuade people to be generous in giving their money to help meet the needs of others when they have been led to believe that the point of religion is that their acts of praise and worship will have the effect of causing God to send blessings that will meet the needs of their own lives? Time and attention must be given to the task of educating and encouraging black middle-class Christians in the area of responsible stewardship.

Responding to the Needs of the Least of These

C. Eric Lincoln offers a keen insight into the challenge of responding to those outside the church doors in *The Black Church in the African American Experience:*

> One advantage that many black churches have is the fact that the majority of them are still located in the ghetto.... Black churches can take advantage of their location and begin the difficult task of organizing these deprived inner-city communities and providing a political voice and community infrastructure; whether they will do so remains to be seen.[4]

Lincoln then recalls a statement from Martin Luther King Jr. in *Where Do We Go from Here?* King says, "It's time for the Negro middle class to rise up from its stool of indifference, to retreat from its flight into unreality and to bring its full resources — its heart, its mind and its checkbook to the aid of the less fortunate brother."[5] That is the recurring message of biblical faith. Will we or will we not respond to the needs of the "least of these" (Matthew 25:40)? Will we sell what we have and give it to the poor (Luke 18:22)? Are we prepared to gain the whole world and still lose our own souls (Matthew 16:26)?

Amos, the prophet of the eighth century B.C., noted that God was not pleased with the noise of our songs. God demands instead that we "let justice run down like water, And righteousness like a mighty stream" (Amos 5:24, NKJV). Micah, another prophet of the same era, echoed a similar message. He declared that God was not pleased with our elaborate acts of worship. What God wants is that we should "do justice and love mercy and walk humbly with God" (Micah 6:8, RSV).

As black people living in America, we are well accustomed to and feel strangely soothed by these words of Scripture directed at rich and powerful white people who seem to us to be unresponsive to our pleas for justice. We must now consider the possibility that these prophetic warnings can rightfully be directed at us by God, out of displeasure with the way we are responding to the needs of the people just outside the doors of our churches. As the black middle class expands and strengthens, we must bear in mind the warning from James Sanders that any reading of prophetic texts that leaves us feeling better about ourselves is probably a misreading. Indeed, the "least of these" are probably not seated on the pews next to us on the inside of our churches. They are more likely to be found sitting on the park benches, sleeping on the heating grates, and eating out of the garbage cans of our inner-city areas. And they are turning to our churches every day for aid, assistance, and compassion.

The mandate is clear. If the black middle-class church is to be responsive to the needs that exist in the inner-city areas where such churches are located, responsible stewardship is a necessary component. And stewardship must be defined not only in terms of the amount of money the church encourages its members to bring in but also the amount of the operating budget the church is committed to dispersing to people and programs that do not touch the life of the congregation. Only then can the black middle-class church be sure that it does not stand condemned by the parable of the rich man and Lazarus. This is not merely a story in the Bible. This is the reality that awaits every black middle-class Christian worshiping in an inner-city congregation as we come in and out of our churches. God will surely judge us, not in relation to the songs we sing, the sermons we preach, or the prayers we offer inside our churches to and for each other. God will judge us, according to Luke 16, based upon whether or not we notice Lazarus standing outside our door and pause to address his needs and acknowledge his humanity.

Giving as We Have Received
Titus 3:1–7

A STUDENT AT ASHLAND SEMINARY RECENTLY TOLD ME the story about a man named John, one of his neighbors, who had recently purchased a riding mower with which he could cut the grass around his home in a rural part of the state. John had been told that the bill for the purchase of that riding mower would arrive in the mail in a few days, and so every day he looked through the mail expecting to see the invoice. He was, apparently, very prompt and dutiful when it came to paying his bills, and he did not want his payment to be late. However, after more than two weeks, the bill had still not arrived.

John then took it upon himself to simply send a two-hundred-dollar payment through the mail, and he attached a note indicating that the check should be applied against his balance from the purchase of the riding mower. Much to his surprise, a response from the company came within a few days. The envelope did not contain the invoice that he had been expecting. Instead, his check was returned to him with the surprising comment that, according to the company's records, he had a zero balance.

Certainly there was some mistake, thought John, and so he sent another check to the company, and he attached a note suggesting that there must be some computer error and that he was certain that he still owed the company a considerable amount of money for the riding mower. A few days later, another letter arrived from the company. Once again, the check was enclosed, and the company assured John that their computers were very accurate and clearly indicated that John had a zero balance.

Most people would have dropped the issue and simply enjoyed their riding mower, courtesy of the company that assured them that they owed no money. However, John was apparently not like most people. Once again he enclosed a two-hundred-dollar check payable to the company, and this time he enclosed a Polaroid photograph of himself sitting on that riding mower. He mailed that letter off, knowing that the next time he heard from the company things would be in order and the proper invoice would be enclosed. Not so! Within a few days, the company responded to John. Once again they assured him that he owed them no money. They thanked him for sending the Polaroid, which they were going to keep. Then they begged

---

This sermon was preached by the author at Antioch Baptist Church in Cleveland, Ohio, on October 3, 1998.

him not to send any more letters or checks. In very large print at the bottom of the page were the words: YOUR ACCOUNT IS PAID IN FULL!

This is a true story about a man named John. In a very real sense, it is also a true story about all of us who have placed our faith in Jesus Christ. Despite the debt that we owe because of our sins, each one of us has received a letter written at Calvary in the rich, red blood of Jesus. The first line says that God loves us. The second line says that Jesus washed our sins away when he hung and died on that cross. The third line says that we have all been forgiven. And down at the bottom, with letters written by the hand of a merciful and gracious God, it says: YOUR ACCOUNT IS PAID IN FULL!

That is the message that Paul writes to his friend Titus, who is serving as overseer of the church on the island of Crete. First, Paul lists an awful array of human sins. Perhaps as we review it we can see which one seems best to apply to our own lives. That is the power of the Bible. It does not focus on any single area of human sinfulness, suggesting that God is concerned only with that particular area of conduct. Instead, the Bible lays out a wide range of human sins and suggests that if one shoe does not fit, perhaps another one does. Listen to this list and see if anything fits.

Paul says that, at a certain point in our lives, we were foolish or immature, disobedient toward God and enslaved to various human lusts and passions. The list goes on to suggest that once we were filled with malice and bitterness, consumed by envy, and filled with hate toward one another. I appreciate hearing this list because it reminds me that sexual sins are not the only sins that are of concern to God. I wonder how all the people who want to impeach Bill Clinton would compare if they laid their lives down next to Titus 3:3?

Is there anyone here today who has not had a struggle with being foolish or disobedient? Is there anyone here who has not had to wrestle with passions and lusts for things you know you should not have? Is there anyone here who has never had to battle against the impulses of malice or envy or hatred? In fact, Titus 3:2 warns us not to speak evil about other people but to be gentle and show meekness, because we too once lived and walked in sin.

Then the hand of mercy reached down and touched us. Then the love of God went forth and saved us. Then the grace of God was poured out to redeem us. We were not saved by our own righteousness, says Titus 3:5. We were saved by the mercy of God, which was poured out upon us in abundance. This is the same message that Paul delivers to the Ephesians when he says, "For by grace are ye saved through faith; and that not of yourselves: it is the gift of God: not of works, lest any man should boast" (Ephesians 2:8–9, KJV).

Paul then goes one step further than our modern-day story about John. After all the letters had been exchanged between John and the company that made his riding mower, all that John ended up with was a riding mower. After the transaction at Calvary, you and I end up with quite a bit more. Not only have our sins been erased, but also we have become heirs according to the hope of eternal life (Titus 3:7). You and I who are so quick to criticize and condemn the sins we see in the lives of others really should not say a word. Our own sins are so numerous and, sometimes, so glaring that we have no room to talk about anybody else.

Nevertheless, God has acted through Christ not only to take away the penalty that we should have had to pay for those sins, but also to guarantee us a spiritual inheritance that we begin to enjoy now. Then, by God's grace, we continue to enjoy that inheritance even after death when we are called to live with God in heaven. In other words, not only do we have a zero balance as far as the penalty for our sins is concerned, but we actually have a credit in the bank of grace against which we will be able to draw both now and later. All of this God has done for us, says Paul in Titus 3:5, because of God's kindness and love.

In light of what God has done for us, I want to ask what we should be willing to do for God – not in return, but in response. Let me borrow a line from the songwriter Andrae Crouch, who raises the question: "How do I say thanks…?" One thing we can do is look at our level of stewardship and see if it really reflects an awareness of just how much God has done for us. We can look at our regular support of the ministries of this church, and we can look at our level of support for the Nehemiah Project and ask ourselves if we are giving in proportion to how we have received.

I believe that stewardship is something that is best understood in the context of the grace of God. We should not give our time, talent, or money to the church simply because the pastor asks us to do so. We should not give in response to an appeal made by a human voice. We should look at our past disobedience, foolishness, envy, malice, hatred, and lusts. Then we should hear the voice of God say to us: "You have a zero balance!" In fact, we need to hear the voice of God say, "I have made you an heir to eternal life." Then, in light of what we have received *from* God, we should give back *to* God.

We should give, not in the hope that something good might happen as a result. I can remember the Watchnight services on New Year's Eve when I was on the staff at Abyssinian Baptist Church. Many times the local gamblers and numbers bankers would come to church and make a generous contribution. They came to church only on that one night of the year. They were not even CME Christians (Christmas–Mothers' Day–Easter). They came out to give money on New Year's Eve because they believed it would result in good luck in the coming year.

That is not how we should give to the church, hoping that something good will come to us in return. Our giving should be based upon the exact opposite principle. We should give because of what we have *already* received. God has already been good. God's grace has already been sufficient. The blood of Christ has already been shed. Our sins have already been forgiven and washed away. We have already been made heirs of salvation. And so we give because so much has been given to us despite our long, ugly, sinful past.

Take a look at your stewardship today. Does it reveal a person who is giving in response to how much God has done for you? Or does your stewardship look like a story I heard from one of my friends the other day? He said that most of the members of his church wake up on Sunday inside $100,000 dollar homes. They get dressed in $500 suits and $300 dresses. They wear $100 shoes and $50 neckties. They check the time on $500 watches while they drive to church in $30,000 automobiles. They take off their $2,000 minks and their $500 leather or cashmere coats. All of this they do so they can proudly place one dollar in the collection plate. They then go out after church to eat a fabulous meal, having invested less in the work of God on that day than they spend on the tip they leave for their server in the restaurant or than they pay for their Sunday newspaper. It is my hope and prayer that nobody here is reflected in that story. People who know how much God has done for them are willing to be generous in support of the work that goes on in God's church.

Take a good look at your stewardship today. Does it remind you of this story I heard over the summer? A certain preacher said that the twenty-dollar bill and the one-dollar bill were having a conversation. The one-dollar bill asked the twenty-dollar bill where she had been traveling lately. The twenty-dollar bill said proudly, "I have been to the finest restaurants, the best hotels, the most fabulous clothing stores, and the most exotic vacation locations." The twenty-dollar bill then asked the one-dollar bill where he had been traveling. The one-dollar bill lowered his head and said dejectedly, "Oh, you know, the same old place. Church – church – church." Is that the nature of your stewardship or mine today? Do we take our twenty-dollar bills to those places where they can be spent on ourselves, being careful to bring our one-dollar bill to church on a regular basis? Take a look at your stewardship today.

Let me give you another reason to be generous in your stewardship. In Matthew 25, Jesus says that you and I will ultimately be judged not on the strength of what we do for ourselves, but on the strength of what we have done for "the least of these." He defines "the least of these" as the hungry, the homeless, the sick, the imprisoned, the poor, and the lonely. Come to this church during the week, when all of our fine cars have left the parking lot. Come and see the people who live in this neighborhood walking through these doors for the hunger program, for the AA program, to drop their children off for free Head Start, or in search of some needed assistance. That is the real ministry of this church.

Consider the people who are shut-in over a long period of time. Their contact with this church is through the radio broadcasts, the tape ministry, the cable TV programs. Six days every week, sometimes twice a day, the message of the gospel goes out to the world from this church. Who knows how many lives are being helped? Who knows how many souls are being reached? We do not gather at Antioch for the sole purpose of speaking to the people who are able to show up physically. We have a message to share with the world. Do you think that your stewardship is sufficient to help us get that message across? It is not for ourselves only that we maintain this church, but also for the sake of "the least of these." Take a good look at your stewardship.

Think of the needs that we still need to address. The number one health hazard in most urban, African American neighborhoods – like the one in which this church is located – is AIDS. Whether contracted through drug use, sexual conduct, or a blood transfusion, AIDS is a disease that is spreading most rapidly among our people. Do not say that it cannot happen to you or your family. Increasingly, AIDS is being transmitted within marriage unknowingly when one spouse, who has been unfaithful or otherwise becomes infected by a third party, infects the other marriage partner. We need to provide space and resources so that victims of AIDS and their families can be assisted. We need to provide space and resources so education and AIDS prevention can take place before people contract this silent killer.

All of this is the Nehemiah Project. It is hunger centers and AA meetings in rooms that provide adequate space. It is Head Start in a space that is secure. It is reaching out with the Word of God to touch the souls of people. It is reaching out with a human hand of compassion to touch the lives of those who are "the least of these." Look at your stewardship. Are you bringing one dollar with you when you drive to this church in your thirty-thousand-dollar automobile? Do your twenty-dollar bills see all the best places while your one-dollar bill is reserved for church? Do you acknowledge that God has been good to you? And if so, is your stewardship a reflection of your gratitude? Do not give your money because you want God to do something for you in return. Give because you know how much God has already done. *Give as you have received!*

Chapter 7

Worship: Bridge or Barrier within the Black Church?

The LORD is in his holy temple;
let all the earth keep silence before him.
— *Habakkuk 2:20, RSV*

Make a joyful noise unto the LORD, all ye lands.
Serve the LORD with gladness:
come before his presence with singing.
— *Psalm 100:1–2, RSV*

HAVE BEEN A MEMBER OF BLACK MIDDLE-CLASS CHURCHES in urban settings in the Midwest and on the East Coast for more than forty years. I have been the pastor or served on the pastoral staff of four such churches over the last twenty-nine years. One thing has remained constant from one church setting to the next during all of that time, and it is the question of how we shall worship God in this place. In most instances, the challenge seems to be choosing between the high-spirited and expressive worship styles commonly associated with the Southern black religious tradition and the more restrained forms of singing, preaching, and praying that many black churches may have adapted from their encounters with mainline white churches. Shall we encourage everyone in the church to "make a joyful noise," or shall we seek a more hushed environment in which worshipers are encouraged to "keep silence" in the presence of God? This question of how to engage in the worship of God is, or has been, a point of tension within every black middle-class congregation with which I have ever been acquainted.

The Historic Forms of Black Worship

Writing in 1903 in an essay entitled "Faith of the Fathers," W. E. B. Du Bois observed that black religion at the turn of the twentieth century was defined primarily by three things: the preacher, the music, and the frenzy.[1] Albert Raboteau in *Slave Religion* argues that those same three things defined most black religious gatherings among slaves in the nineteenth century as well, though he added a fourth component to the list — the emotional impact of conversion.[2] In James Baldwin's 1952 novel *Go Tell It on the Mountain*, all four of these components are examined, both in the rural South and in a Pentecostal church in New York City in the 1940s.[3]

More often than not, when black religious life is discussed or depicted in any of the performing arts, it is the exuberance, the emotion, the energy, and the occasional moments of ecstasy that are featured. This was true in such stage productions as *Purlie, Your Arms Are Too Short to Box with God*, and *Abyssinia*. It was true in television programs that focused on the black religious experience, such as *Amen* in the 1980s and 1990s and segments of *The Flip Wilson Show* in the 1970s. Such films as *Nothing But a Man* (1964), *Hallelujah* (1929), *Once upon a Time When We Were Colored* (1996), *A Time to Kill* (1997), and *The Color Purple* (1985) all feature sequences of a black worship experience that reflect all of the expressiveness described earlier. However, as a way of pointing to the tension that occurs within black middle-class congregations, consider the film *The Vernon Johns Story*. This 1990 film about the man who preceded Martin Luther King Jr. as pastor of Dexter Avenue Baptist Church in Montgomery, Alabama, in 1950 is illustrative of those black middle-class churches that have intentionally sought to leave behind all forms of expressiveness in worship.

Socioeconomic Status and Worship

Why has the question of how to worship become so controversial in some black middle-class congregations? Perhaps it is because the expressive and emotional forms of worship are associated either with memories of slavery or with life in the South, both of which many upwardly mobile black people wanted to escape and forget. Wyatt Tee Walker reminds us that the original function of black worship was to assist black people to survive in white, racist America. Walker asks the question, "How is it that this black community has been able to resist and weather, over and over again, the continuous assault on our personhood inflicted by the systemic racism of American society? The answer, undoubtedly, is the nature of our religious faith."[4]

Whether during slavery, the bleak years of Jim Crow, or in the northern ghettos to which black people fled during the great migration, the black church was largely "a balm in Gilead" for the wounded and weary souls of black people struggling just to survive in America.

The question then becomes what happens to the forms and functions of black worship, which served us so well in earlier days, when our socioeconomic position begins to improve, we leave poverty behind us, and we move into the middle class? The answer seems to be that as black people begin to assimilate into white society, many of them struggle with whether or not they should abandon their historic forms of worship in favor of a more restrained and nonexpressive experience.

In *Black Metropolis*, Horace Clayton and St. Clair Drake described how the upward mobility of black people was reflected in their church affiliations:

> When a person in Bronzeville [Chicago] says that he is sanctified or that he attends a Spiritualist church or one of the cults, he is immediately marked down as "low-status." If a man says he's an Episcopalian or Congregationalist, Bronzeville thinks of him as "dicty" or a "strainer" or "Striver." But if he says he's Baptist or Methodist or Catholic, he can't be placed until he tells what congregation he belongs to.[5]

This analysis of black life in general and black religious life in particular, written more than fifty years ago, continues to be a relevant analysis of class distinctions within the black community. How we shall worship God — or whether we will continue to worship God at all — as our socioeconomic status improves and our access to mainline white society expands is a pressing question.

In an attempt to present a different face to society, many black middle-class congregations intentionally seek to restrain all forms of expressive worship that have been employed by black people since the days of slavery. In many such churches, Negro spirituals are no longer sung. Gospel music is also not performed, whether from the contemporary sounds of Richard Smallwood and Kirk Franklin or from the earlier era defined by Mahalia Jackson and Thomas A. Dorsey. People are discouraged from saying "Amen" in response to the preaching or the singing and receive a look of shock and displeasure if they break with the practice of worshiping in silence.

The "holy dance" of the Pentecostal and Holiness churches is ridiculed as excessive emotionalism. The rich instrumentation of storefront churches that employ tambourines, guitars, drums, horns, and rhythmic hand clapping is never heard. Neither are the long-meter hymns that blend the words of European hymn writers like Isaac Watts and Charles Wesley with the call-and-response musical tradition, which reaches back to West Africa centuries before slavery.

Expressiveness — Not Just a Black-Church Issue

Henry Mitchell, writing in *Celebration and Experience in Preaching*, makes the important point that the tension between expressive and nonexpressive forms of worship is not unique to the black church in America. He notes that similar tensions existed in the white church of the nineteenth century during the evangelistic efforts of Charles Finney in the "Burned Over District" of upstate New York and of the twentieth century during the "sawdust trail" crusades of Billy Sunday throughout the country.[6] Standing behind these two examples are the contrasting styles of the Anglican and Presbyterian churches of eighteenth-century America and the zeal of the Baptist and Methodist preachers of the First Great Awakening along the eastern seaboard.

Charles Chauncy, a Congregationalist minister, delivered a classic sermon on the dangers of "enthusiasm" in preaching in 1742. He warned his Boston congregation against the "fashionable practice of flocking to hear only those ministers whose gifts were for warm and zealous preaching."[7] Then Chauncy went on to accuse the Enthusiasts of ignoring the dictates of reason, of engaging in wild physical movements, of being the victims of a disease, a sort of madness, of not operating under the power of the Holy Spirit, of being as divisive to the eighteenth-century church as were the men in 1 Corinthians who claimed to be with Apollos or Cephas or Paul.[8]

The dean of an Episcopal seminary in Pennsylvania recently preached in the chapel at Ashland Theological Seminary. He noted that he was mindful of the difference between the liturgical approach to worship in his tradition and the enthusiasm that was the mark of worship in the chapel that morning, which he associated with the seminary's Wesleyan and German Pietistic heritage. To make that point more forcefully, he recalled a tombstone of an Anglican prelate he saw in a cemetery near Cambridge, England. That tombstone read, "By the grace of God he preached the Gospel of Jesus Christ for forty years without enthusiasm." That was a clear reference to the Anglican-Methodist feud that led to John Wesley's alienation from the Anglican Church of his youth after his "heart was strangely warmed" during a German Pietist service in England in 1738.[9] That tension still exists within the white church in the United States. Most mainline white denominations have abandoned expressiveness in worship. Not only do they not encourage worshipers to say "Amen" during the service, but often in their rush to be finished with the service within one hour, they do not give the worshipers any reason to do so.

I shall never forget preaching in the Gothic chapel of an Ivy League university in the 1980s — and being told that the service must be completed within forty-five minutes. There was no room for any variation from the printed order of service. The sermon had to be completed within fifteen minutes. The time for prayer was prescribed, with no time for silent meditation or reflection in the presence of God. I wondered to myself if the benefactor of that magnificent chapel meant for the worship services to be so perfunctory. The whole experience seemed to be driven by a greater interest in what was going to happen after the service than by anything that might happen during the service. A sense existed that order was of greater importance than feeling, that watching the clock was of greater urgency than waiting on the Lord. Unfortunately, what I experienced in that university chapel service is what happens in many mainline white congregations across the country. One wonders how often people leave such worship experiences confessing, "My heart was strangely warmed."

Contrast my chapel experience with the spirited and highly energized services associated with the Assemblies of God churches or with many of the ministries broadcast over various cable TV networks. That celebrative side of the white church in worship has also been captured in the arts. One thinks primarily of Steve Martin in *Leap of Faith* (1990), Robert Duvall in *The Apostle* (1997), and Dan Akroyd in the TV series *Soul Man*. The most notable of all such representations of the white worship experience would be *Elmer Gantry*, in both the 1927 novel and the 1960 film.

While expressiveness in terms of emotion is not the issue, there is a struggle within the ranks of the Roman Catholic Church regarding how to worship. Since the church moved away from the exclusive use of Latin during the Mass in 1928, Catholicism has been searching for new ways to worship God. Charismatic groups have arisen within the Catholic Church. The use of gospel music has become common. The length and importance of the homily is being reconsidered. Still to be resolved is the more difficult question of the ordination of women as priests able to administer the sacraments of the church.

American Judaism is also engaged in the question of the right way to worship God. The tensions among the Orthodox, Conservative, and Reformed branches of Judaism are real and divisive. How precisely shall sabbath laws be observed? What does it mean to be a kosher family, both in terms of what is eaten and how it is prepared in the home? Must a prayer shawl be worn? Must men and women be seated in separate sections? Must the leather straps that bind replicas of the Torah around the arms and the head be worn? These are not issues of expressiveness, but they do point to a general principle. The struggle over how to engage in worship is not a topic exclusive to the black church. It has, in fact, occupied black and white Christians in Europe and America and Jews around the world for more than two hundred fifty years.

Black Worship as a Fusion of Many Influences

With this in mind, it is important to point out that black worship, even in its most expressive forms, is not entirely the creation of black people. Rather, it has always been an amalgam of influences. In black worship, one can see and hear aspects of European hymnology, West African traditional religion with the use of call and response, slave songs, American frontier music and evangelical zeal, and the charismatic and Pentecostal fervor flowing out of the Azusa Street Mission under William Seymour at the turn of this century.

This being the case, the solution to the problem of how worship should take place in black middle-class churches does not have to lie in allowing the historic forms of black worship to be entirely lost. It is not necessary for black worshipers to assimilate into some emotionless experience that seems to justify itself by alleging that it exalts reason over enthusiasm, mind over heart, and quietude over celebration. Rather, the answer lies in the intentional blending of various strands of worship into the life of the congregation. The blending can be done within a single worship service in which various musical forms are presented. This can also be accomplished by varying the theme and content from one week to the next, so that a different face is presented each Sunday. Moreover, blending worship forms in the congregation can also be done by offering different approaches at various set services during the week: for example, offering a traditional service at 11 A.M., a service that takes on a different character at 8 A.M., and a midweek service that offers yet another opportunity to reflect diversity in forms of worship.

The Evolution of Expressive Worship in One Black Middle-class Church

When I arrived at Antioch in 1987, that congregation had the reputation of being a place where worship was largely nonexpressive. The first thing I heard from fellow pastors upon my arrival in Cleveland was, "You'd better not say 'Amen' or shout in that church." The worship atmosphere of the church was not as bad as the rumors on the street would have had me believe, but there was more than a little truth to the rumor that the worship experience was cold and formal.

People who did say "Amen" or who "answered back" during the preaching were met with steely glances and were told to "shhh" by people who held fingers up to their lips. Frequently the expressive worshipers would even be approached after the service and asked what was wrong with them for "making all that noise." Not long after my arrival, as I urged people to become more expressive in worship, I received a letter from a church member who harshly reprimanded me for trying to tamper with "the traditions of Antioch." She told me that she had chosen that church forty years earlier because she preferred to worship God "in quiet dignity." That woman, now long deceased, would probably not remain at Antioch today. Another member predicted that if I continued down the path I was pursuing, Antioch would end up being "just another nigger Baptist church." Needless to say, the class contempt inherent in that statement was revealing. The problem I faced, however, was that the churches that some in Antioch held in scorn were growing in membership, while our membership had long since leveled off. Something had to be done if our congregation was to remain viable, and I determined that worship was where we were going to begin.

In 1987 the music was primarily anthems and hymns, though Negro spirituals were regularly sung by one of the choirs. The service was governed by the printed order of worship, and departures from the standard order were not well received. The length of the service was closely watched, and when I went beyond the traditional end time of 12:30 P.M., that fact was unequivocally brought to my attention. Antioch was clearly locked into a pattern of worship defined by Habakkuk 2:20: "let all the earth keep silence before him."

I was convinced that our worship service was the greatest obstacle to our continued growth as a congregation. It was comfortable for the members of our aging congregation, but it did not make us attractive to new families who were visiting various churches while looking for a new church home. I did not think we had to throw out the formal aspects of worship. On that point, I am in agreement with J. Wendell Mapson Jr. in his book *The Ministry of Music in the Black Church*. Although his book focuses upon the place of music in the service, it speaks equally well to the whole of the service. He writes, "Music in the black church must balance the freedom of the Holy Spirit with liturgical restriction. Spontaneity must be tempered with a sense of order and meaningful content. Emotion in black worship must be affirmed, but emotionalism must be discouraged."[10] I was interested in establishing such a balance in our worship life so that over the course of time the worship service would offer something for everyone.

We gradually succeeded in bringing some overt praise into the service and encouraged people to be more expressive and vocal during the service. A new choir specializing in modern gospel was formed; it eventually incorporated many of the old standards from the repertoire of gospel music. We added an electronic keyboard and a drum machine to the sounds of the pipe organ. There was some initial resistance when the new choir began to "sway" as they sang. It surfaced again when they introduced a tambourine one Sunday morning. Those were sights and sounds that many in the congregation had not experienced in their lifetime.

We added a devotional period fifteen minutes before the start of the Sunday morning service, which had been a time when many of the old hymns were sung a cappella. During this new devotional time, members are invited to stand and give personal testimonies, make prayer requests, and simply offer praise to God. The key to this is a worship leader who is able to warm up the congregation, no matter how cold it may be, through the warmth and enthusiasm of his or her own zeal and faith. We are blessed to have Deacon Tilmon Brown, whose joy in the Lord is contagious and whose singing and praying gifts are invaluable to the congregation.

Other adjustments were made to the worship service itself. We now solicit prayer requests from the congregation prior to the pastoral prayer. We frequently hold altar calls, when people come to the front of the sanctuary, hold hands, and agree to pray for one another. Carefully chosen, the music during the prayer time always seeks to reflect the black musical repertoire. Such hymns as "In the Garden," "Sweet Hour of Prayer," "Precious Lord," "Amazing Grace," "I Need Thee Every Hour," "Have a Little Talk with Jesus," "Beams of Heaven," and others set the spiritual mood in which our prayer life is rooted.

The 11 A.M. service now regularly extends to over two hours, and attendance at that service has steadily increased. We have also added an 8 A.M. service. It too is informed by these principles of worship.

Special Days and New Worship Forms
Black middle-class churches can take full advantage of special services during the course of the year to inject diversity into the worship life of the congregation. It can start with those Sundays when Communion and baptism take place. There are many songs as old as the presence of black people on American soil that can be sung while candidates are being led to the place of baptism or while the Communion elements are being distributed or received. "Take Me to the Water," "Wade in the Water," "Let Us Break Bread Together on Our Knees," and "Were You There" are just a few of the songs from the black musical traditions that can be used during the services.

The church can do something special with music and preaching themes on the Sunday before Martin Luther King Jr. Day. "We Shall Overcome" comes to mind, as does the song that was its source — "I'll Overcome." Other appropriate songs are "Oh Freedom," "Go Down Moses," "I Shall Not Be Moved," "If I Can Help Somebody," or "Only What You Do for Christ Will Last." Such musical selections can be accompanied by sermons that focus on such themes as justice, courage, faith, love, self-sacrifice, the equality of all persons, the cost of discipleship, and the ever expanding list of heroes of the faith as found in Hebrews 12.

Since February is Black History Month, I have had good success in using the Sundays in that month to focus on music and composers we may not use throughout the rest of the year. In the past, we have devoted whole services to the music of Thomas A. Dorsey, Charles Albert Tindley, and Andrae Crouch. We have also woven an entire service — sermon and music — around the lyrics and historical / biblical lessons of certain Negro spirituals, such as "Steal Away to Jesus" and "Couldn't Hear Nobody Pray."

Music as Key to a Balanced Worship Experience
I recommend that churches seek variety in their musical offerings, not only from week to week but within the same service. Choral preludes and postludes offer two different opportunities to employ varying musical traditions. Processional and recessional hymns can be drawn from different traditions as well. Our sanctuary

choir, which specializes in singing from the European anthem tradition, makes an effort to sing a Negro spiritual every time they lead the worship service. We are one of the few churches in Greater Cleveland that makes a conscious attempt to keep alive the musical genre of Negro spirituals. It is a part of our history and culture that must be preserved and passed on to successive generations of Christians, black and white.

At Antioch, we also rotate among three adult choirs for the first three Sundays of each month. A choir that specializes in traditional gospel music from such composers as James Cleveland, Shirley Caesar, and others from the years 1930 to 1960 sings on the first Sunday. A choir that concentrates on modern gospel artists such as Richard Smallwood and Kirk Franklin sings on the second Sunday. The sanctuary choir (anthems / spirituals) sings on the third Sunday.

The fourth Sunday is devoted to two children's choirs: the cherub choir, whose members are ages 2–12, and the young people's choir, who are 13–18 years of age. These two choirs concentrate on contemporary praise songs but also become a way by which the young people learn the hymns of the church. Including the children in leadership in the worship service not only turns them from spectators to participants but also brings out their parents who might not otherwise be in church that day. The children's choirs have become one of the primary ways by which we nurture and cultivate the spiritual lives of our young people. A fifth Sunday, when it occurs, is the time when the male chorus sings, typically offering variations of well-known hymns.

There is, of course, an advantage that comes with having multiple choirs in a congregation, but the same effect can be achieved through the use of a single choir that has been trained to sing more than one genre of music. That is the case with such great church choirs as Abyssinian Baptist Church in New York City and Bethany Baptist Church in Brooklyn. The six years I spent between those two congregations, 1970–76, were instrumental in any success I have subsequently had in ministry. Both of the congregations are rich in the vitality of their worship, made possible in large measure by the genius and imaginativeness of their world-class preachers: William A. Jones, Samuel D. Proctor, and Calvin O. Butts III. However, one cannot discount the incredible breadth of musicianship resident within their primary choral groups and instrumentalists.

The Centrality of Pastoral Support in Increasing Expressiveness

It has been my experience that if the church is to reflect diversity in worship and to break away from a nonexpressive approach, the leadership of the pastor is essential. No one else is better positioned to affect the planning of the worship services. No one else is better positioned to influence the work of those who head the music ministry. And no one else is better positioned to provide whatever instruction and biblical teaching may be required to move a congregation toward a more balanced approach to worship. If the pastor is not interested and is not willing to invest some effort in the process, bringing about such changes in worship will be much more difficult to achieve.

Henry Mitchell is very insightful at this point. He says,

> There exists a widespread, often unconscious, and rigid opposition to rejoicing in the presence of God, as an act of adoration. The conscious and unconscious restraints of the preacher-liturgist are contagious. Thus the pastor dare not complain that the congregation simply does not loosen up, when in fact the main source of inhibition in worship may well be in the pulpit.[11]

More often than not, black middle-class churches have pastors who are eager to bring about greater balance and established members of the congregation who do not want to follow his or her lead. Such a change in worship is almost unfathomable if the roles are reversed and the pastor does not want to make that move. When such a scenario is the case, the pastor must be encouraged to give more room to the movement of the Holy Spirit. It will invigorate the worship service, result in spiritual and numerical growth in the congregation, and provide an environment in which the preaching of the gospel will be greatly aided and empowered.

Black Worship as a Combination of Three Essential Elements

Up to this point, I have hinted at the role that music, prayer, and preaching play in black worship. However, emphasis has been placed upon the role that diversity in music plays in contributing to an increased expressiveness in some black churches. In most middle-class churches, it is the music, as shared both by the whole congregation and by a choir or soloist, that most frequently results in expressiveness in the worship service. Melva Costen writes about the centrality of music in the black worship experience:

> The African American community is traditionally a singing community. African Americans are a people of faith who sing jubilantly of God's loving presence in the midst of struggle. Like the early Christians, we gather in song to proclaim Christ's identification with us. Like our African forebears, we sing with our total beings in praise of the Almighty God by the power of the Holy Spirit.[12]

In most black churches, the energy, enthusiasm, and exuberance discussed in this chapter is rooted in and the result of the music ministry.

Yet there is more than music that must be considered when discussing worship in the black church. I have already noted Du Bois's 1903 observation about the role of music, frenzy, and the preacher.[13] In a helpful treatise based upon his 1983 Hampton Ministers Conference Lectures, Wyatt Tee Walker offers a more contemporary analysis of the essential ingredients in the worship life of black churches. He says,

> It is my view...that in Black Worship there exists three primary support systems, *preaching, praying* and *singing.* These are not the only ingredients, but certainly, the essential ingredients. Authentic Black Worship does not proceed unless these three ingredients are present and operative in some fashion.[14]

I agree wholeheartedly with Walker. I would suggest that adequate attention be given to how all three of these areas can be employed to bring balance to the worship life of a congregation that has been resistant to any of the forms of expressiveness that have long been associated with the black church.

To that end, I conclude this chapter with a sermon entitled "The Reasons We Worship God." What this sermon does is not just demonstrate a sermon that might have the effect of generating expressive responses from the congregation. More importantly, this sermon will serve as an example of how to share with a congregation the meanings and methods of Christian worship. It is the assumption of this sermon that black middle-class churches can be nurtured and instructed in ways that can and will result in transforming them into communities of faith that "make a joyful noise unto the Lord."

The Reasons We Worship God
Psalm 100

EXPERTS IN THE FIELD OF NUTRITION ADVISE US THAT IN order for the human body to reach and sustain maximum health, we need to eat foods drawn from the various food groups. When I was a younger person, I always thought the food groups included equal amounts of hamburgers, French fries, soft drinks, and dessert. I later learned that the actual groups included meats, vegetables, fruits, and bread. A balanced diet drawn largely from these food groups will, we are assured, result in improved health, energy, and fitness.

It should not come as a surprise that there are basic groups from which we need to draw if we are to reach the maximum level of spiritual fitness. We need to feed our souls with the same care that we bring to the feeding of our bodies. And we need to be equally concerned about a proper balance in our spiritual diet. There are five areas in which all Christian need to be engaged if they are to reach maturity and maximum spiritual development.

We need, I would suggest, a good amount of prayer and Bible study so that our inward character is being shaped. We need a good amount of repentance and confession of sin so that we remember that we cannot point our fingers at the sins of others because God is not yet through with us. We need stewardship and discipleship so that we are giving of our time and resources to advance the work of God in places both local and beyond. Finally, we need worship so that we constantly remember the great, awesome, loving, and faithful God, whose actions on our behalf make him worthy of our praise.

Today it is worship that will occupy our time and attention. We need to engage in the worship of God on a regular basis, and we need to fully understand why that worship is so deserving. We need to do exactly what Psalm 100 states. We should, in the words of the King James Version, "make a joyful noise unto the LORD." We should "come before his presence with singing." We should "enter into his gates with thanksgiving and into his courts with praise." And I want to stress the key words in this psalm. They are "joyful noise," "thanksgiving," "singing," and "praise."

I know that for some people *worship* is understood primarily as reverence, silence, and quiet reflection. I know that for some people right here

---

The author delivered this sermon at Antioch Baptist Church in Cleveland, Ohio, on February 7, 1999.

Chapter Seven

in Antioch, worship is not about emotion or energy or exuberance; rather, it is about what one of our members said to me in a letter about ten years ago when she said that worship at Antioch is defined by "quiet dignity." I do not doubt that there are times when silence is the order of the day. I agree with Habakkuk 2:20, which says, "The LORD is in his holy temple; let all the earth keep silence before him" (RSV). However, this verse deals with recognizing the difference between true and false gods, not how we should worship. That verse says that the idols made by human hands from wood or stone or metal have no power. However, the God of the Bible is the one true God who demands our respect and worship. These words tell us that God is worthy of being worshiped, but they do not mean to suggest that the worship must be done in silence.

Think about a courtroom when the people are mingling and talking among themselves, and suddenly the judge walks into the courtroom. What happens? People stop talking, rush to their seats, stand in silence, and remain there until the judge is seated and invites them to sit. At that point the proceedings begin. That is what Habakkuk is suggesting. When you come into the presence of God, you ought to acknowledge God's holiness, majesty, power, and glory. God is greater than we are; be silent. God is wiser than we are; be silent. God is holier than we are; be silent. We see this very same thing in the impeachment trial, now nearing an end, of President Clinton. Whenever the chief justice of the United States Supreme Court enters the Senate chamber, everyone present stands in silence, out of respect for that office. That is all Habakkuk is suggesting.

However, once you have acknowledged the greatness of God, it is time to worship and praise him. It is my contention that once you begin to remember not only who God is but also what God has done for you in your life, you cannot remain silent very long. One gospel song puts it this way:

> When I think of the goodness of Jesus,
> And all he's done for me,
> My soul cries out hallelujah,
> Thank God for saving me!

Look at Psalm 100, therefore, as offering two invaluable lessons. The first is why we should worship God, and the second is how that worship should be offered.

Let us first consider the meaning of the word itself. What does it mean to worship? The *Holman Bible Dictionary* suggests that worship is what happens when you find yourself in the presence of the divine. Worship involves certain practices, occurring in certain places and being done in a certain spirit. Let us conclude that worship is what helps us separate God from everybody and everything else in the world. I may respect other people, but I worship only God. I may honor a certain political or academic or ecclesiastical office, and the person who holds that office, but I worship only God. Only God is worthy of praise. Only God is deserving of bending our knees and humbling our hearts. Many of us shook hands with the president of the United States when he visited this church in 1994, but I heard nobody shout out, "Hallelujah." Worship is the act that separates God from everything else in all of creation.

Let Psalm 100 tell us, first of all, that God is worthy of our worship. It says, "Know ye that the LORD he is God: it is he that hath made us, and not we ourselves" (KJV). This is enough to cause us to worship God. We are not self-sufficient people. We are not independent characters. We did not cause ourselves to be born, and we cannot prevent ourselves from dying. We have been made by the hand of God. We have been animated by the Spirit of God. We wake up every morning by the grace of God. We eat food from the earth because of the faithfulness of God, who sends rain and sun. He is God, and he made us and the world in which we live.

The psalm also tells us that "we are his people, and the sheep of his pasture" (KJV). God has agreed to adopt us into his family and to provide for us as a shepherd provides for the sheep. I do not know about you, but I draw tremendous reassurance from Psalm 23, which reminds me that "the LORD is my shepherd; I shall not want." Sometimes God will lead me into pleasant times in green pastures and still waters. Sometimes God will lead me into places where everything is calm and still and my soul can be at rest. The Lord is my shepherd.

Other times I am assured that when I find myself in the valley of the shadow of death, I am not alone because the Lord is with me. Notice that when God does the leading, the destination is always pleasant – green pastures and still waters. God does not lead us into the valley of the shadow of death. God does not lead us into the presence of our enemies. But when the shifting circumstances of life draw us into dangerous territory, God does promise to join us in those places so that we do not have to make that journey by ourselves. The Lord is my shepherd.

Either way, God deserves to be worshiped. We ought to worship God because he does allow us to enjoy days of peace and rest. In this wicked world with all of its sins and dangers, God does build a fence around us. And even when the world breaks through in the form of danger or death or disaster, God is still with us providing the faith and strength to carry on. That is what we mean when we sing these words by Horatio G. Spafford:

When peace, like a river, attendeth my way,
When sorrows like sea billows roll –
Whatever my lot, Thou has taught me to say,
It is well, it is well with my soul.

It is good to be one of the people of God. It is good to be a sheep in his pasture. I might add that in Psalm 100 we are warned against self-worship as well. There are some people who think they are the greatest thing on earth. I would imagine that all of us know such people. They think so highly of themselves, they leave you with the impression that they think they are God. Like the pharaohs of Egypt and the caesars of Rome, they hold a dangerous illusion. I had a college classmate who fell into this problem of self-worship. He came from Syracuse, New York. He would walk across the campus at night with a flashlight in his pocket. As someone would approach him on one of the sidewalks, he would remove the flashlight, turn it on, and hold it over his head. Then he would say, to the absolute amazement of those who passed by, "I'm so fine, I just have to stop and check myself out." Then while the flashlight was still on, he would invite the person to take a good look at him because, he said, "It is certain to be the best sight you are going to see today." My friend had a serious case of self-love.

In Greek mythology there was a god, named Narcissus, who fell in love with his own image. He ended up dying because he could not bring himself to see or notice anything but his own reflection. He was the epitome of self-love. There remain to this day people who are essentially narcissistic. They love themselves above all else. They forget that their beauty or handsome features will soon fade away. They forget that the rugged health they now enjoy can leave them as quickly as a thief in the night can rob them of their worldly goods. It is a dangerous thing to love ourselves too much, because we are essentially unreliable. We cannot help ourselves when we need that help the most. That is why Psalm 100 reminds us that we worship God because "The LORD he is God: it is he that hath made us, and not we ourselves." It is God who has saved us and not we ourselves.

Verse 5 reminds us that only God deserves to be worshiped because only God has qualities that are absolutely unique. The psalmist lists three such qualities, and I would like to mention each of them briefly. First, we worship because God "is good." Second, we worship because "his mercy is everlasting. Third, we worship because "his truth endureth to all generations."

Let each one of these reasons for worship sink into your mind and heart today, and you will quickly conclude that only God deserves to be worshiped.

I say without hesitation today that God is good. I agree with those who say, "God is good all the time, and all the time God is good!" I don't know about you, but God has done nothing but bless my life. God has put no obstacles in my path; he has moved them out of my way. God has not caused me to sin; he has washed my sins away. God has not required me to go hungry through this world; he has found a way to put food before me. God has been my doctor when sickness hovered near me. God has been my deliverer when danger and even death moved in to claim my life. I can say with Psalm 27, "I had fainted unless I had believed to see the goodness of the LORD in the land of the living" (KJV).

Will anyone here today be a witness about the goodness of the Lord? Will anyone here today bear witness to the fact that when you were sick, God raised you up? Does anybody here know that when every door seems shut tight in your face, God can and will make a way out of no way? Is there someone here who has to worship God today because you know that he has been good? Whatever we accomplish in life is not because we have been successful, but because God has been faithful. I praise God today because he is good. I shout "Hallelujah" today because God has been good. I worship the Lord today with my whole heart because God has been good.

However, the psalmist does not leave us with this broad and general notion of goodness. Instead, he takes us into a deeper dimension of the goodness of God. The writer says that part of the goodness of God is tied to God's mercy. We can worship God because "his mercy is everlasting." Several months ago, Deacon Rambo handed me a little note that helped draw a distinction between grace and mercy. The note said, "Grace is getting what you don't deserve, while mercy is not getting what you do deserve." I need grace and mercy. I worship God, first because he gives me things I don't deserve. God sent his son to die for me. I don't deserve that. It was grace. God has prepared a place for me in heaven. I don't deserve that. When I come to the end of this life and my body is laid in a grave, that will be only temporary housing. One bright morning my grave will be rocked by the power of God. I will be raised from death to life. I will be caught up to meet Christ in the air, and I will forever be with the Lord. I don't deserve any of that. It is grace.

While grace is getting what I don't deserve, mercy is not getting what I do deserve. I am a sinner. I deserve to spend an eternity in hell. I deserve to be taken into the sanctuary of Satan and be cut off forever from the presence of God. That is what I deserve. But somebody else died in my place. Somebody else paid the price for my sins. Somebody else laid down his life on the cross at Calvary so that I could lay claim to eternal life in glory. Praise be to God; that is mercy.

Chapter Seven

Last month Pope John Paul II visited Missouri. While he was there, he asked the governor of Missouri to grant a pardon to a man named Darnell Mease, who was sitting on death row for a triple murder. The governor, who is a defender of capital punishment, granted the pope's request and commuted the man's sentence from death to life without parole. That is mercy. However, you and I can be the recipients of a greater mercy than that. There was a time when we were sitting on a spiritual death row. "The wages of sin is death; but the gift of God is eternal life," says Romans 6:23 (KJV). God showed mercy upon all of us. He commuted our death sentence. But God does not sentence us to life without parole. Instead, he sentences us to life abundant and eternal. We worship God not only because God is good but also because his mercy is everlasting.

Finally, we worship God because his truth endures to all generations. Just last Friday morning in the Bible class we were discussing this idea of "the truth of God." Over and over, especially in the writings of John, the question of "the truth" comes up: "You shall know the truth, and the truth shall make you free" (John 8:32, NKJV); "I am the way, the truth, and the life: no man cometh unto the Father, but by me" (14:6, KJV). Jesus said to Pontius Pilate, "Every one that is of the truth heareth my voice." Pilate answers Jesus with one of the most haunting questions of all time: "What is truth?" (John 18:37–38, KJV). In 2 John 1:1–2, this idea of "the truth" comes up again. There seems to be an urgency attached to the idea of knowing and walking in and believing the truth of God.

Why is there such value attached to the truth of God? Psalm 100 tells us it is because the truth of God is the only thing that lasts forever. All other ideas and notions of men and women come and go. People used to believe that the earth was the center of the universe and that the sun revolved around the earth. No one believes that any longer. People once believed that the earth was flat and that if you sailed far enough, you would drop off the edge of the earth into hell. No one believes that anymore. Not one of the ideas of men and women lasts forever. But the truth of God endures to all generations.

The current issue of *Time* magazine has a cover story about hip-hop music. It has been twenty years since rap music emerged in New York City and then Oakland. It may have seemed as if that music would take America by storm. But while it is still around, look at the changes. Tupac Shakur and Biggie Smalls were shot to death. M. C. Hammer and Vanilla Ice have vanished from the rap scene. The Sugar Hill Gang is over the hill. Lauryn Hill, the current queen of hip-hop music, was quoted as saying that she is writing music "that will be around forever." A nice thought, but just like the song that said, "Rock and roll is here to stay," so too will this music and its singers come and go. Nothing fashioned by human hands or minds will be around forever.

However, there will always be somebody singing to the glory of God because his truth endures forever. It will always be true to love God with all your heart, mind, soul, and strength. That truth will last. It will always be true to love your neighbor, as you love yourself. That will always be true. The Ten Commandments will always be true. The Sermon on the Mount will always be true. The promises of God will always be true. The equality of all persons, providing for the needs of the weak and the poor, working to end oppression in all of its forms, all of this will always be true. The truth of God endures to all generations. This is that "old time religion" that was good enough for my dear mother and is good enough for me.

The words of the Bible will always be true. Think of how old this book is, and yet we turn to it regularly for direction in life. The most recent parts of the Bible are almost two thousand years old. The oldest parts are well over 3,800 years old. Think of all the books written during those years that nobody reads any longer. Think of all the books that no longer even exist. They have vanished from the face of the earth. Yet, after all these years, the Bible is still being printed. The Bible is still being translated into new languages. The Bible is still being read. The Bible is still being trusted. The Bible is still comforting. The Bible is still guiding. The Bible is still feeding the hungry souls of men and women. That is because the words of the Bible point us to that God whose truth endures to all generations.

Note the word *endures*. Let the sense of struggle and having to overcome rest upon you. People have tried to disprove the Bible, but it has endured. Scholars have tried to discredit the Bible, but it has endured. In some places, it was made a crime to be found reading the Bible, but it has endured. The power is not in the book. The power is in the person to whom the book points. This is the Word of God, and it lasts forever because God lasts forever. And we worship God because his teachings, his word, his revelation, his truth, endureth forever.

Chapter 8

To White Churches with Black Middle-Class Members

Other sheep I have, which are not of this fold…
and there shall be one fold, and one shepherd.
—*John 10:16, KJV*

BETWEEN 1977 AND 1986, I WAS THE PASTOR OF ST. PAUL Baptist Church, a black middle-class congregation in Montclair, New Jersey. It was an all-black fellowship in a town that was predominantly white. We had an interracial clergy fellowship that met on a monthly basis, and it was at one of those meetings that the issues to be discussed in this chapter first began to take shape. During one of the meetings of that interracial fellowship, I first came to grips with the issues that are generated when black people affiliate with predominantly white congregations.

During the meeting, I made a flippant remark about "black people who drive past solid black churches in order to worship with white congregations." A white Presbyterian pastor in the group took great offense at my comment, though he did not reveal his feelings at that time. Instead, he invited me out to breakfast and shared his feelings at great length. He wondered aloud if I doubted that he had the ability to be an effective pastor to the many black members of his predominantly white congregation. He wondered aloud whether black people had the right to affiliate with white churches without having their motives challenged or their racial loyalties questioned. There was much about black life he did not understand.

The Black Middle Class and the "Afro-Saxon Mind"

I attempted to share with my white colleague the long history of black people who do leave or bypass black churches in favor of white churches because they do not want to be identified any longer with black people. Calvin Marshall, in an essay entitled "The Black Church — Its Mission Is Liberation," discusses this tendency and traces it to what he calls "the Afro-Saxon mind":

> Many black people in America and the Caribbean are suffering from what I choose to term the Afro-Saxon Mentality. These people usually think of themselves as being middle class and in many instances tend to be more affluent than the average black. . . .
>
> In America some of the symptoms of those who are suffering from this disease are pre-occupation with getting out of the black ghetto and into integrated neighborhoods, joining interracial churches, country clubs, yacht clubs, etc. In short, achieving all of the status and success symbols of the white community.[1]

That was not an uncommon practice in Montclair or within any other black middle-class community in America. In fact, many of the second- and third-generation black residents of that town actually referred to themselves with great pride as BASPS (Black Anglo-Saxon Protestants).

A fuller treatment of the Afro-Saxon mind is found in *Our Kind of People: Inside America's Black Upper Class* by Lawrence Otis Graham.[2] This book deals with so-called black society, that group identified with Jack and Jill, the Links, the Boulé, and the various Greek-letter societies. It is not uncommon for persons in this group, when they attend church at all, to join interracial, even predominantly white, congregations. This was a history and a set of social issues with which my friend was completely unaware.

The Historic Shape and Content of Ministry in the Black Church

I tried to explain my view that the black church has played a historic role in the life of the black community that goes beyond offering traditional forms of pastoral support. The black church has also offered advocacy on the social issues that impact the lives of black people and a community of support that shelters and soothes black people in their daily struggles with white racism. The black church has also been the base where much happens in the way of community organizing. Political candidates are screened; civil rights groups come to spread their message and solicit financial and volunteer support. The black church has served as a repository of various aspects of black culture, including the Negro spirituals, certain preaching styles, long-meter hymns, the observance of Black History Month, and much more.

It was my concern that while a white pastor could preside at a wedding or a funeral as effectively as a black pastor, the white church was neither positioned to nor had shown itself interested in meeting the other needs and challenges that confront black people. These are matters that are paramount in the ministry of black churches. Thus, the question was not simply should black people be free to join white churches, or can white church leaders provide effective pastoral care. The real question is whether white churches, pastors, and lay leaders are conscious of the world in which their black members must live outside of the sanctuary and whether they will be responsive to that reality.

The Challenges Faced by White Churches with Black Members

Will white churches preach a gospel message that seeks to comfort their black members as they contend with racism and injustice in their daily lives? Will white churches challenge their black members to assume an active role in addressing the array of social, educational, and economic issues that continue to have a negative impact on those black people who remain locked in the inner cities? This is an important consideration since many of them came to such churches to escape that reality. Will white churches be able to assist their black youth to grow up with a fully developed sense of self-identity and self-esteem, as discussed in chapter 3?

Will white churches use their economic resources to empower the agencies and institutions whose mission it is to support the aspirations of black people? That would include such groups as the United Negro College Fund, the National Association for the Advancement of Colored People (NAACP), the National Urban League, and local black arts institutions. Will white churches invest a portion of their financial resources with black-owned banks and credit unions? Will they contract with black-owned small businesses for a variety of services including building maintenance, insurance, printing and paper products, security, and office machines and supplies?

All of this is what the black church has historically done, and my concern, as voiced more than twenty years ago, is whether white churches would do the same as a way of responding to the presence of black members within their congregations. The issue is not black membership; the issue is the ministry a white church is willing to conduct in response to the presence of its black members. A failure to make such an adjustment is a clear indication that the black member is simply being further assimilated into white society and is being further cut off from the black community.

The White Church and Black Members: Past and Present

I reminded my white colleague that his predecessor at that same church had been an outspoken supporter of busing to achieve racial integration in that town's school system. One Sunday he preached on that topic, and the next week the congregation voted to remove him from his position. Is it enough that the pastor is compassionate and open-minded when the bulk of the congregation remains hostile to black people, unmoved by the aspirations that sustain them and the issues that concern them?

I am fully conscious of how this view can be interpreted as black racism, and that is clearly not my intention. I am not challenging the right of black people to affiliate with white churches. They have been doing that since Richard Allen and Absalom Jones held membership in the St. George Methodist Episcopal Church in Philadelphia, Pennsylvania, in 1787.[3] Rather, I am seeking to challenge white congregations to be fully supportive of and responsive to the hopes and humanity of its black members. That has been the major problem since Jones and Allen walked out of St. George Methodist Episcopal Church in that same year and formed the first church in America for free black people.[4]

I have never been able to escape the irony of the fact that in Philadelphia in 1787 the United States Constitution was being drafted with its reference to black people being counted as three-fifths of a person.[5] At that same time, and in that same city, black people were also being treated as second-class citizens in the house of God. The issue that has concerned me is not whether black people should join white churches. That is a choice they are perfectly free to make. The issue is also not whether white churches will receive them into membership. The issue is whether white churches will offer a ministry to its black members that comforts them in light of their afflictions rooted in their being black in America.

At the same time, will the white churches afflict their black members when they become too comfortable with their own condition and show no interest in "the least of these"? And perhaps most important of all, will white churches direct their financial resources, their membership network, and their moral authority to address and ameliorate the social and economic issues that may be of importance to their black members? It is not until the issue cuts at the level of the distribution of congregational resources, and the process by which such decisions are made, that the responsiveness of white churches to the presence of black members can be fully determined.

The Continuing Problem of Racial Segregation in the Church

I remember the troubling comment made by Liston Pope in 1960 that "the most segregated hour in American society is 11 A.M. on Sunday morning."[6] Martin Luther King Jr. referred to that reality in his 1963 "Letter from the Birmingham Jail." It is frequently forgotten that what prompted King to write that historic and stirring treatise on liberty was the harsh criticism leveled against him by the white interfaith clergy of that community.[7] He goes on in that letter to reflect upon the nature of white Christian churches that not only denied membership to black people but also actively opposed their attempts to gain their freedom.

I am well aware of the fact that rarely, if ever, do white people seek membership in predominantly black congregations. I am also aware of how rarely a white congregation will select a black person to fill the role of senior pastor. James Forbes at Riverside Church in New York City is one of the exceptions to the rule. The life and ministry of Howard Thurman should also be recalled at this point. He was a black preacher who served between 1953 and 1964 as dean of the chapel on the predominantly white campus of Boston University. Thurman also attempted to establish and served as senior pastor of an interracial congregation in San Francisco between 1945 and 1953.[8]

The Rise of Black Denominations in the Nineteenth Century

The question of black leadership in white congregations was at the heart of the dispute in the eighteenth century involving Richard Allen, Absalom Jones, and the Methodist Episcopal Church. Blacks were accepted as members, even as preachers; however, they were required to sit in a segregated section of the sanctuary.[9] Their experience was repeated when James Varick and Peter Williams led another group of black people out of the John Street Methodist Church in New York City in 1796. They left their church because black members were not allowed to come to the chancel rail to receive Communion at the same time as white worshipers.[10] That proved to be a segregation within the church of an even more offensive nature.

When Jones and Allen separated from the Methodist Episcopal Church, it was this issue of segregated versus integrated worship that subsequently caused them to choose different paths. Absalom Jones led a group of black people in forming a congregation within the predominantly white Episcopal Church of America in 1795, becoming the first ordained black Episcopal priest in the United States.[11] Meanwhile, Richard Allen was unwilling to deal with being under the control of a predominantly white body of church overseers and set in motion the formation of the first black denomination, the African Methodist Episcopal Church (AME). He became its first bishop in 1816.[12] Varick and his followers in New York City took an approach similar to that of Richard Allen, organizing the AME Zion Church in 1823.[13]

Black People and White Churches in Postmodern America

More than two hundred years after Allen, Jones, and their colleagues walked out of that church in Philadelphia, the presence of black members within predominantly white congregations remains one of the most delicate areas in American church life. It seems apparent to me that as black people continue to experience upward mobility, they will move into neighborhoods farther and farther away from inner-city churches and established black communities. Many within this group, in keeping with the current discussions about a postmodern world where membership within a religious community has become of less importance, will not join any church at all. For those black people who do move away from the cities and from black communities, some of them will decide to attend the local white congregation near their new home. That will be far easier for them than traveling some greater distance back to the city or to the black church nearest to where they now live.

It is the assumption of this book, however, that most black middle-class Christians will continue to make that journey back to the city, no matter where they may choose to live. They will do so because they want to maintain their affiliation with their childhood congregation. They will want to expose their children to that environment on the grounds that the church may be the only setting in which their children will be exposed to black culture, black institutional leadership, and a majority black institution. Many black middle-class people travel great distances to attend black churches because they want to share in the substance and spirit of the black worship experience that is harder, if not impossible, to find in most white churches. Thus, the bulk of this book is written with the assumption that most black middle-class Christians will continue to affiliate with predominantly black churches, most of which will be located in the inner city.

However, there is every reason to assume that an increasing number of black people will seek membership in predominantly white suburban congregations, with white leadership at the clergy and lay level. This chapter is not interested in discouraging them from making that move. Again, many black people in this country have been attempting to worship God in an interracial setting from the time they were introduced to the Christian faith during the Great Awakening. Rather, this chapter seeks to challenge those white congregations to become settings in which the spiritual, social, and emotional needs of black members can be adequately addressed.

The Experience of Black Congregations in White Denominations

There is some additional history that can be drawn upon as we consider the presence of black members in predominantly white congregations. Over the last thirty years, many black pastors and lay leaders have expressed frustration over what seemed to them to be their second-class status within largely white denominations. They were ordained members of the United Presbyterian Church, the United Methodist Church, the Disciples of Christ, the United Church of Christ, American Baptist churches, the Episcopal Church in America, and the Roman Catholic Church. Despite their membership and ordination in the church, these blacks have been allowed to exercise little leadership in their denominations and have expressed great frustration. There has been anger over the reluctance of the white church to take more of a leadership role in the civil rights movement. There were pain and disappointment over the investment portfolios of the white churches that helped undergird the racist regimes in South Africa and Zimbabwe (Rhodesia). And there was general frustration over what was viewed as the institutional racism manifested by local and national white church bodies.

This frustration eventually took on institutional form in such groups as the National Committee of Black Churchmen, which issued its first statement on July 31, 1966, at the foot of the Statue of Liberty.[14] That pronouncement was followed by *The Black Paper*, which was written by a group called Black Methodists for Church Renewal.[15] This was a black caucus within the United Methodist Church that issued its statement at a national gathering of that church body in February 1968. One of the most dramatic expressions of the frustration that black Christians felt toward the white church came from the National Black Economic Development Conference, which sponsored James Foreman's *Black Manifesto*. This document was presented at Riverside Church in New York City on May 4, 1969, when Foreman walked in and took over the morning worship service.[16]

On April 18, 1968, the National Office of Black Catholics issued a statement from the Black Catholic Clergy Caucus that began with this dramatic statement:

> The Catholic Church in the United States, primarily a white racist institution, has addressed itself primarily to white society and is definitely a part of that society. On the contrary, we feel that her primary, though not exclusive work, should be in the area of institutional, attitudinal and societal change.... This is a role that white priests in the black community have not been accustomed to playing and are not psychologically prepared to play.[17]

In every case listed above, the issue was not the appropriateness of black people holding membership in white churches or in being part of an all-black congregation in a predominantly white denomination. Instead, the issue was how responsive those white churches were prepared to be as regards the issues that were important to their black members.

Several notable books of sermons and related statements also emerged from that era. Black preachers seized the opportunity to speak their concerns. The books include *Black Preaching: Select Sermons in the Presbyterian Tradition; Black Gospel/White Church*, which comes from black Episcopal priests; and *Out of Mighty Waters: Sermons by African-American Disciples of Christ Pastors*.[18] I must also mention the gripping autobiographical statement *Black Priest/White Church: Catholics and Racism* by Father Lawrence Lucas.[19]

This dissatisfaction with the white church that bubbled to the surface in the above-mentioned documents at the end of the 1960s took on another significant form: black theology. James Cone, the leading voice of that theological movement, cast the issue most clearly in his first book, *Black Theology and Black Power:*

Black Power is Christ's central message to twentieth-century America. And unless the empirical denominational church makes a determined effort to recapture the man Jesus through a total identification with the suffering poor as expressed in Black Power, that church will become exactly what Christ is not.[20]

Cone continues his discussion by stating that as of 1970 the white church in America had fallen far short of this kind of ministry. He says,

The white church has not merely failed to render services to the poor, but has failed miserably in being a visible manifestation to the world of God's intention for humanity and in proclaiming the Gospel to the world. It seems that the white church is not God's redemptive agent, but, rather, an agent of the old society. It fails to create an atmosphere of radical obedience to Christ.... It not only failed to preach the kerygmatic Word, but maliciously contributed to the doctrine of white supremacy.[21]

It is for white churches throughout America to respond to these accusations from Cone. My own suspicion, however, is that these charges continue to be true in many white congregations across the country.

Black Members as Leaven inside White Churches

The presence of black members within white churches, a phenomenon far more prevalent now than it was thirty years ago, may serve as the motivation for white churches to assume a more active role in addressing the lingering issues of racism, poverty, and disadvantage. Hopefully, the black members will be aggressive in challenging their predominantly white churches to direct their financial and human resources and their moral authority toward programs and projects that serve to address and relieve human need within their surrounding community and, when possible, across the country.

Black people within white congregations can be like leaven in a loaf of bread, helping good things to rise to the surface from within. Should the black members fail to offer direction and encouragement to their white churches to join in the struggle for human rights, or should white churches fail to heed the invitation of its black members, then I fear that my concern voiced more than twenty years ago will remain in force. Richard Allen and Absalom Jones walked out of the white church because it was not supportive of, or responsive, to their presence. Those things would have to change in order for black people to affiliate with white churches without being seen as merely assimilating deeper into white society.

The Black Middle Class and the Reach of Racism

I end this chapter with a reminder that there is no neighborhood in which black people can move where they can finally and forever escape racism, even if they have become entrenched in a white church. That is all the more reason those white churches must be conscious of and responsive to this issue as far as its black members are concerned. Four events that occurred or were reported in February 1999 help bring this issue into focus. In Chicago, it was reported that when black middle-class people began moving into the once exclusively white Ashburn neighborhood on the city's southwest side, white families almost immediately began moving out. Census data reports that "in Chicago and its suburbs at the beginning of the 1990s, only 110 of 1,169 neighborhoods could be described as integrated, or 10 percent to 50 percent black. By the middle of the decade, only 27 of those 110 remain integrated."[22] This resistance to neighborhood integration in Chicago, which was at the heart of the 1958 play *A Raisin in the Sun* by Lorraine Hansberry, remains an issue today.

What will white churches in the communities into which blacks are moving be willing to say about the continuing problem of white flight? Or will the white church eventually leave that community as well? That is what happens in most instances. White Protestant congregations have all but abandoned the cities of America, dutifully following their members into the suburbs and away from the poverty, the problems, and the people of urban America. And those white churches that have not yet moved out of the city are, in too many cases, silent in the face of the issues of injustice that surround them.

The second event took place in New York City. It involved a young black man from Guinea named Amadou Diallo, who was shot to death by four police officers who fired forty-one shots at him while he was cornered in a doorway in the Bronx. This tragic event, coupled with other instances of police brutality in that city, caused G. Michael Bellinger, a member of the black middle class, to write an editorial to the *New York Times* entitled "Why I'll Be Marching with Sharpton." He wrote, "Although a card-carrying liberal African-American, I confess to an increasingly conservative lifestyle: practicing law at a large mid-town law firm, monitoring my internet stocks, wondering if the weather will interfere with my tee times." As a result of the shooting of Amadou Diallo he found himself saying, "I can no longer take refuge in a luxury high-rise and ignore the trampling of the rule of law by those hired to serve and protect us all."[23] Here is a member of the black middle class who was enjoying the good life and yet came to realize that he could easily be the next victim of random police brutality. Any white church with which Bellinger, or any other black person, might affiliate must be sensitive to this fear of random violence and the racist sentiments that produce it. And such churches should ask themselves whether or not they are willing to speak up and condemn such acts when they occur, whether they have black members or not.

The third event points to a crime concept sadly termed "driving while black." This refers to any young black person, typically male, who may be pulled over and harassed by the police simply because he is driving a late-model luxury car. The assumption is that the car may be stolen because there is no other reason a young black male would be in such a vehicle. There was a case of this very thing in Cleveland reported in the *Sun Press* on February 18, 1999.[24] A twenty-year-old black male was beaten and maced by four members of the Cleveland Police Department after he had been pulled over because the police suspected he was driving a stolen car. A computer search revealed that the car had not been stolen, and the young man had broken no law.

Many members of the black middle class, myself included, are made to worry about the safety of our own sons when they drive our cars because the local police may assume them to be guilty of the crime of "driving while black." White churches must be sensitive to situations like this and must speak out against them when they occur, if they are going to be supportive of their black middle-class members.

The fourth incident occurred in Oakwood Village in suburban Cleveland, Ohio. This community is home to a rapidly growing community of black people who have moved out of Cleveland in search of their first home or who are looking for a larger home with more land and better schools. A local barber had a bulletin board outside his establishment that announced, "February Is Black History Month!" One evening that sign was defaced, and a racial slur was written in place of the word *black*. The mayor and the local police were contacted, and neither showed any interest in the matter. That caused great consternation within the black community, who may have thought they had left such racial animosities behind them.

That incident brought to the surface a series of other racial incidents that had occurred in that community within recent days. Local black pastors attempted to call press conferences and galvanize public opinion around the issue of racial diversity and against racial intimidation. There was not one white church in Oakwood Village, or any of the surrounding communities, that was willing to stand with the black pastors and condemn the acts that had occurred.[25] These black people had moved into $200,000 homes; however, they soon discovered they had not moved away from racism or racial discrimination.

Has the White Church Changed since 1787?

Black people may join white churches, but what will they receive that will help them survive in this society with dignity and self-esteem? That was the question that confronted Richard Allen and Absalom Jones in 1787. They left St. George Methodist Episcopal Church in Philadelphia because although they could hold membership, the church did not embrace their full humanity. How much different will it be for black people in white churches in the year 2000 and beyond? I do not doubt that black people will continue to affiliate with white churches for various reasons. Nor do I want to discourage black people from doing so. Instead, I want to challenge white churches with black members to speak a healing word to their black members who come to church having battled the still prevalent forces of racism and discrimination in American society. I want to challenge white churches to urge their black and white members to be fully involved in programs that help those who remain impoverished, imprisoned, and infirmed in this society. Finally, I want to challenge white churches, whether they have black members or not, to direct their congregational and institutional resources toward the shaping of a more just society.

A Concluding Statement about Black and White Churches

Black people have come a long way in this country over the last two hundred years, but there still remains a long way to go. That distance can be traveled more quickly, and equal opportunity can be secured more rapidly, if two things can occur. First, the white Christian community must stand up and be counted when instances of injustice or institutional racism occur. They must do this especially when they have black members in their congregations. But they should do this even if their membership has no blacks at all, because it is consistent with the mandate of the gospel.

Second, the black middle-class church located in the inner cities of America cannot simply be worship centers for those who commute in from the suburbs on Sunday, looking past and walking by Lazarus who sits outside their church door. Such churches must recognize that they have two congregations. One gathers weekly for worship and fellowship and provides the funding through their tithes and offerings. That congregation needs comfort in the face of continued racism and the other burdens of life that money cannot remove. They need constructive criticism so that they do not become so caught up in secular values and social organizations that they marginalize the role of the church in their lives. And they need a continual exposure to the riches of black culture as they are resident within the music, songs, and prayers heard and experienced in black worship.

The other congregation gathers every day of the week, often unknown and unseen by those who drive in and out on Sunday. This second group gathers in need of food, help in meeting financial emergencies, counsel in coping with addictions, and advocacy with the bureaucracies of government that they encounter on an ongoing basis. The black middle-class church has within it the financial and the human resources to meet much of this need and the moral authority to help advocate for societal change that can remove their root causes.

It is clear what must be done in shaping a relevant and comprehensive ministry to the black middle class, whether that ministry takes place within a black or a white congregation. What remains is for the work to begin where it has not yet started and to be continued in those places where it is already under way. It is my hope that pastoral and lay leadership in such churches will be helped and guided in their ministries, one way or the other, by the thoughts and suggestions set down in this book.

The problems that confront us are great, and we must respond quickly, for time is of the essence. We dare not simply wait and watch while events in our cities and throughout our society unfold. God will surely judge us by the things we are prepared to do right now in and through our churches.

Taking a Stand for the Lord
Ephesians 6:10–18

MANY THINGS RELATED TO THE TRAGIC SHOOTINGS IN Littleton, Colorado, continue to sadden and trouble my soul. There is the simple fact that fifteen people, including the two gunmen, were shot to death. There is the planning that went into the event where over five-hundred people were targeted for death through guns and explosive devices. There is the reality of parents who did not know that their children were building bombs in the garage and who did not take enough precautions to keep their children from getting hold of guns. There is the callous attitude of the National Rifle Association (NRA) that went ahead with its convention in Denver, celebrating the right to own guns when guns had just torn the heart out of that community two weeks before.

I read with great interest the editorial by Orlando Patterson, a Jamaican-born Harvard sociologist, who wondered what the national response to these events would have been if the shooters in Colorado had been black, inner-city youth, instead of affluent whites from the suburbs. He notes that in each of the five or six school shootings that have occurred in this country over the last two years, all of the shooters have been white. However, notes Patterson, society is not prepared to give up on white teens. But when one black youngster takes one life, tragic as that is, there is suddenly a national debate about what is wrong with black youth.

I must confess that when the events in Littleton were first reported, I held my breath, hoping that no black child had gone on a shooting rampage. It was clear to me from the outset that the shooters were not black, however, because if they had been, that would have been said right away. You would have heard something like, "Murderous black teens...." What you heard instead was, "Youths in black trench coats..." with no reference to race or color. Orlando Patterson is right; the awful legacy of racism in America is apparent even in the way crimes are reported.

It is disturbing that we as a nation do not see the connection between the way a country solves problems and the way our children follow that example. Every day, without fail, there is a stream of news reports about bombings and missile attacks in [the former] Yugoslavia and occasionally in Iraq. We show pictures of refugees who report unspeakable violence. We confess that some of our planes mistakenly attack innocent civilians.

This sermon was delivered by the author at Antioch Baptist Church in Cleveland, Ohio, on May 1, 1999.

We have not *declared* war in Yugoslavia, but we are certainly waging a war. Why are we surprised when the children who see war on TV every day, and who play video games that simulate war and shooting, suddenly act out what they see adults doing? What makes matters worse is that life is no better for the people in Kosovo. We have not been successful in making it safe for them to stay in their own country. They have no homes to which to return when the fighting is over. More than likely we will be asked to help pay to rebuild the very same villages that have just been destroyed.

By the way, where is the $6 billion coming from that Clinton needs to fight this war? Do we just happen to have that much money lying around, or are we taking money from much needed domestic programs so that we can shoot $1-million missiles that frequently miss their targets? When will we learn what Dr. King said during the Viet Nam war and what Jesus said almost two thousand years ago – that when you live by the sword, you will surely perish by the sword? Please ask yourself whether the violence in Columbine High School in Littleton, Colorado, is not an extension of the almost constant state of war that America has been in since 1776?

Perhaps the most chilling thing that happened in Columbine High School took place when one of the shooters asked one of the students whether or not she was a Christian. In the midst of that gruesome and terrifying scene, that student had no way of knowing why such a question was being raised. If she said yes, would her life be spared? If she said no, would they put a bullet into her skull? What would you have said or done in such a situation? Those who were inside the school report that the young girl answered without hesitation, "Yes, I believe in God. I am a Christian." Immediately she was shot and killed.

Looking back on that event, we might ask ourselves the question, If she had said no, would her life have been spared? Was she going to be killed no matter what she said? We will never know what was going on in her mind, and we will also never know what was in the minds of the two boys responsible for her death. But one thing we know with certainty: under the most stressful circumstances you could possibly imagine for young high school students, this young woman stood up for Jesus. "Yes," she said, "I believe in God. I am a Christian."

This is exactly the kind of courageous testimony and witness called for by Ephesians 6. We are challenged to "put on the whole armor of God...that [we] may be able to withstand in the evil day, and having done all, to stand" (Ephesians 6:11,13, KJV). *Standing* suggests what we do initially; it points to our early attempts to be faithful to God. *Withstand* suggests that once we stand up the first time, Satan may attempt to push us back from our

Chapter Eight

position. Now we have to hold the ground on which we stand. We have to withstand.

I like that image because it demands that all of us must respond for ourselves. You cannot speak for me, and I cannot answer for you. We must, as individuals, speak up and stand up for ourselves. And what the events in Littleton have taught is that you never know what the response from others will be once you declare where you stand. Maybe you will place yourself in danger, like that young woman. Maybe, because you are afraid of what might happen and you want to avoid that unknown consequence, you will deny believing in God, even deny three times, as Peter did, being a follower of Christ.

However it comes, sooner or later, someone in this world will call you out. Someone will ask you what you believe. You will be asked if you are a Christian, a churchgoer, and a believer in the Bible. And that issue will not simply be raised here in the church. Instead, someone on your job, in your school, among your social acquaintances will bring it up. That person will probably not pull a gun on you, but even so the question will be a test of character, to see how you answer when issue finally comes up. Are you prepared to stand up for Jesus? It will not be easy, but it will be necessary, because as Jesus says in Matthew 10:32, "If you do not own me before men, I will not own you before my Father and the angels in heaven" *(paraphrase)*.

Let me suggest, first of all, that standing up for the faith requires the same thing that physically standing up requires from a baby. It does not happen right away. It takes some time for a baby to gain the strength, the balance, and the coordination to stand up. It is in the child's mind long before the act is physically possible. Many of you have seen babies struggle with this effort to stand up. They crawl around for a while, and then they start trying to pull themselves up, leaning on furniture, or on the sturdy leg of some adult. Then they hold on while they try to steady themselves, leaning and rocking on their short weak legs. But they have a determination to stand up on their own two feet, and so no matter how many times they may rise and fall, they keep trying until they finally are able to stand up. It does not happen all at once. The process is gradual, but the baby does not rest until it has been accomplished.

The same principle is true for us as Christians. God does not expect us to stand up and speak for him when we are still so young in the faith that we do not have any legs beneath us. There is a time when all we need to do is learn about Jesus, grow in the faith, and become increasingly mature in our understanding. But there does come that day when every believer has to pull himself or herself up and take a stand for the Lord. That stand may not require you to answer the direct question of whether or not you believe in

God and in Jesus Christ. As often as not, the test will come when someone attempts to get you to do something that is un-Christian or to leave undone something that every Christian should do.

I remember crossing such a bridge when I was a college student. It was the day after the assassination of Martin Luther King Jr. Several students in the Campus Christian Association were planning a memorial service, and several of us in that group were on our way to the planning session. I happened to be the only black person in that small group that was walking across the campus. On the way we passed a dorm where about six black students were standing. As we passed by, they called to me and said that I should not be seen in the presence of white people because " 'they' had just killed Dr. King." I tried to reason with them, noting that blaming all white people for what one white person had done made no more sense than blaming all black people for what one black person had done.

But they would have none of that. I was immediately labeled an Uncle Tom by people who thought that the appropriate way to mark the death of Dr. King, who had spent his whole life calling for racial integration and moving beyond the sins of the past, was to isolate ourselves into an all-black clique and harbor our hostilities toward white people. These people had never been on a single march, sit-in, pray-in, or other public demonstration in the pursuit of justice. But on that day, they were going to attempt to define for me what my response to the death of my friend was going to be. It was time to take a stand. Either I would kowtow to them and violate everything that Dr. King stood for, or I would go on to that planning meeting with those white students and run the risk of being held in contempt by those black students. Needless to say, I went on to the planning meeting, and we remembered Dr. King in an integrated memorial service that none of the black students who attacked me even bothered to attend.

This is the way it is for Christians in this world. Faith is not just a matter of coming to church on Sunday. It is also a matter of being willing to take a stand, sometimes a controversial stand, for the principles and values that you hold most dear. Among the values that you may hold dear are a genuinely interracial society and a truly integrated body of Christ where people of all races and ethnic backgrounds worship and witness together. That was the value I was trying to stand up for thirty years ago. That is a value that is still worth standing up for today.

However, you and I had better be prepared to lose some friends in the process. This is the lesson of the man after whom Dr. King was named: the sixteenth-century Protestant reformer named Martin Luther. He had been a fervent Roman Catholic priest in Wittenberg, Germany. However, as time went by, he discovered several things about the doctrines of the Catholic

Church that troubled him. In 1517 he nailed a document on the door of the Catholic church in that city containing Ninety-Five Theses, or points of argument. He challenged the authority of the Pope. He asserted the pre-eminence of Scripture over the hierarchy of the church. He argued that salvation does not come as a result of rituals; it comes solely and singularly through faith in the gracious work done by Jesus Christ on the cross. Martin Luther had declared war on the Roman Catholic Church.

Shortly thereafter, he was called before a church tribunal. There officials threatened to excommunicate him from the church if he did not renounce the things he had written earlier. When the time came for him to speak, he offered a defense of his views and opinions. Then, with his relationship to the church hanging in the balance, Luther said, "Here I stand, I can do no other."

I find it interesting that those same words were used by the black artist and political activist, Paul Robeson, who stood against the tyranny of Mc-Carthyism in the 1950s. His autobiography is called *Here I Stand*. Over and over again in history, people have been called upon to stand up and defend what they believe or to stand up and do what they feel God is calling them to do, no matter who thinks they are wrong. Are you prepared to stand when your time comes?

Perhaps the greatest tragedy in life is having nothing in which we believe deeply enough to risk standing up for it. One can recall the words of Dr. King at this point, who said, "If a person has not found something worth dying for, they are not fit to live." Even within the believing community this seems to be the case. Many of us are willing to come into the church and "sit down for Jesus." But how many of us are prepared to venture forth into the rough and tumble of this world and "Stand Up for Jesus?"

That is what Jesse Jackson and his delegation recently did when they went to [the former] Yugoslavia and accomplished through prayer and ne-gotiation what the White House, NATO, and the U.S. State Department could not accomplish through two months of bombing. The risks involved were great. Those people were entering into a war zone, and the bombs continued to fall while they were in the area. The mission could have failed. President Milosevich could have lied to them or even taken them hostage. The whole thing could have been a disaster. It would have been safer to remain in America and call for the release of those three POWs, than to board a plane and take a stand for peace, mercy, and non-violence. But they went, against the advice of Bill Clinton but with the mandate of Jesus Christ that sometimes we must put on the whole armor of God and stand against the wiles of the devil. And having done all, to withstand when you are criticized, vilified, and lampooned.

It must be noted that when you stand up for Jesus you never know who might be inspired by your efforts, even you yourself do not gain immediate success. The power of being a public witness for the Lord is that others will see what you are doing and just might be moved to join in with you and make their own stand for something of great importance. That is what happened in the life of a preacher named Dudley Tyng. That Episcopal clergyman was an ardent critic of the slave trade in America and regularly condemned those in his congregation who were involved in the wicked trade in human lives. After being repeatedly warned about his views and being told that he would be dismissed from his position if he did not tone down his criticisms, Tyng was eventually fired. He assured his opponents that he would continue to preach in opposition to slavery even if he lost his right arm.

Several years later, in a farming accident, Tyng's arm was ripped from his body. After that, his ministry was never able to get back on track. His opposition to slavery had cost him his career. On his deathbed, when he was asked if he had any regrets for the course of action he had taken, he said that the most important thing a Christian could ever do was "stand up for Jesus." Another man, George Duffield heard about the life and the last words of Dudley Tyng, and it inspired him to write a song that has become universally familiar among Christians. That song says, "Stand up, stand up for Jesus, Ye soldiers of the cross!"[26] Dudley Tyng was not successful in his lifetime in bringing an end to slavery, but he inspired many in the next generation. Slavery was abolished, in part by the insistence of those militant Christians who sang these words as their battle cry: "Stand up for Jesus." As it was with Dudley Tyng and George Duffield, so it can be with us today. God wants us to take a stand for something we believe in deeply and to withstand when the world seeks to resist us and condemn us and criticize us for our convictions. Be certain of this, someone else is watching what we do and may be inspired to carry on with the struggle, maybe even taking it to a level we would never have reached ourselves. Standing and withstanding are never easy, but they are necessary. "Stand up, stand up for Jesus!"

Notes

Chapter 1: The Rise of the Black Middle Class

1. Russ Rymer, "Integration's Casualties," *New York Times Magazine*, 1 November 1998, p. 48.

2. William Julius Wilson, *The Declining Significance of Race* (Chicago: University of Chicago Press, 1988), p. 1.

3. *Report of the National Advisory Commission on Civil Disorders* (New York: Bantam Books, 1968), p. 1.

4. James Baldwin, *Notes on a Native Son* (Boston: Beacon Press, 1955), p. 27.

5. Cornel West, *Race Matters* (Boston: Beacon Press, 1993), p. 35.

6. Ibid., pp. 35–36.

7. C. Eric Lincoln, "The Middle Class Mentality," in *Experiences, Struggles, and Hopes in the Black Church*, ed. James S. Gadsen (Nashville: Tidings Press, 1975), p. 61.

8. Henry Louis Gates Jr., "Frontline: The Two Nations of Black America." www.pbs.org/wgbh, p. 1.

9. Harvard Sitkoff, *The Struggle for Black Equality* (New York: HarperCollins, 1981), p. 226.

10. Gates, "Frontline: The Two Nations of Black America," p. 2.

11. Bart Landry, *The New Black Middle Class* (Berkeley: University of California Press, 1987), p. 88.

12. Ibid.

13. E. Franklin Frazier, *The Black Bourgeoisie* (New York: Collier Books, 1957); and *The Negro in the United States* (New York: Macmillan, 1957).

14. Landry, *New Black Middle Class*, p. 47.

15. Frazier, *Negro in the United States*, p. 43.

16. Henry Louis Gates Jr. and Cornel West, *The Future of the Race* (New York: Vintage, 1996), p. 19.

17. Ibid.

18. Clarence Page, *Showing My Color: Impolite Essays on Race and Identity* (New York: HarperCollins, 1996), p. 47.

19. Gates and West, *Future of the Race*, p. 3.

20. W. E. B. Du Bois, *The Souls of Black Folk* (Chicago: A. C. McClurg, 1931), p. 13.

21. Page, *Showing My Color*, p. 57.

22. Ibid., pp. 58–59.

23. Aldon Morris, *The Origins of the Civil Rights Movement* (New York: Free Press, 1984), pp. 1–4.

24. Dirk Johnson, "Jesse Jackson Jr. Is His Father's Son, but He Reaches beyond the Rainbow," *New York Times*, 3 March 1998, p. A10.

25. Dana Milbanke, "Harold Ford Jr. Storms His Father's House," *New York Times Magazine*, 25 October 1998, p. 43.

26. Michael Janofsky, "After Malaise, a New Mood in Nation's Capitol," *New York Times* @aol.com, 11 November 1998, p. A1.

27. Milbanke, "Harold Ford Jr. Storms," p. 43.

28. Wilson, *Declining Significance of Race*, p. 1.

Chapter 2: Confronting Modern Racism

1. A comment made by Derrick Bell at the Cleveland NAACP Freedom Fund Dinner in June 1998.

2. Marvin A. McMickle, "Preaching to the Black Middle Class," *Journal of Preaching* 9, no. 1, (winter 1985): pp. 17–23.

3. Mark Maske, "Off the Field the Barriers Still Stand," *Washington Post* (March 28, 1997), p. E2.

4. Taken from unpublished handouts distributed by Valerie Batts at training sessions in diversity and multiculturalism for the Greater Cleveland Roundtable in 1990.

5. Martin Luther King Jr., "Letter from the Birmingham Jail," in *Why We Can't Wait* (New York: Signet Books, 1964), p. 86.

6. McMickle, "Preaching to the Black Middle Class," p. 18.

7. Randall Robinson, *Defending the Spirit: A Black Life in America* (New York: Plume Books, 1998), pp. 265–66.

8. Peter Paris, *Black Religious Leaders* (Louisville: Westminster / John Knox Press, 1991), p. 19.

9. W. E. B. Du Bois, *The Souls of Black Folk* (Chicago: A. C. McClurg, 1931), p. 196.

10. Paris, *Black Religious Leaders*, p. 21.

11. Edward P. Wimberly, *Pastoral Care in the Black Church* (Nashville: Abingdon Press, 1979); and William Clebsch and Charles Jaekle, *Pastoral Care in Historical Perspective* (Englewood Cliffs, N.J.: Prentice Hall, 1964), pp. 8–10.

12. Wimberly, *Pastoral Care in the Black Church*, pp. 20–21.

13. J. Deotis Roberts, *Roots of a Black Future: Family and Church* (Philadelphia: Westminster Press, 1980), p. 110.

14. Ibid., p. 114.

15. Ibid., p. 116.

16. Ibid., p. 117.

17. C. Eric Lincoln, "Black Church," *Christianity and Crisis* 30, no. 18 (16 November 1970): p. 226.

18. Robert Moats Miller, *Harry Emerson Fosdick: Preacher, Pastor, Prophet* (New York: Oxford University Press, 1985), pp. 251–84.

19. Edmund Holt Linn, *Preaching as Counseling: The Unique Method of Harry Emerson Fosdick* (Valley Forge, Pa.: Judson Press, 1966).

20. Donald Capps, *Pastoral Counseling and Preaching: A Quest for an Integrated Ministry*, (Philadelphia: Westminster Press, 1980), p. 13.

21. Roberts, *Roots of a Black Future*, p. 116.

22. Ibid.

23. Capps, *Pastoral Counseling and Preaching*, p. 15.

24. Wimberly, *Pastoral Care in the Black Church*, pp. 20–21.

25. "Lift Him Up," song by John Oatman Jr., *The New National Baptist Hymnal* (Nashville: National Baptist Publishing Board, 1987), 411.

Chapter 3: Preserving History for the Children of the Black Middle Class

1. John Lewis, *Walking with the Wind* (New York: Simon and Schuster, 1998).

2. Cain Hope Felder, *Troubling Biblical Waters* (Maryknoll, N.Y.: Orbis Books, 1989); and William McKissick, *Beyond Roots: In Search of Blacks in the Bible* (Wenonah, N.J.: Renaissance Productions, 1990).

3. Miles Mark Fisher, *Negro Slave Songs in the United States* (New York: Citadel Press, 1953); and Wyatt Tee Walker, *Somebody's Calling My Name* (Valley Forge, Pa.: Judson Press, 1979).

4. Michael W. Harris, *The Rise of Gospel Blues* (New York: Oxford University Press, 1992).

5. *African American Literature* (Chicago: Holt, Rinehart and Winston, 1992), p. 327.

6. Alex Kotlowitz, *There Are No Children Here* (New York: Doubleday, 1991).

7. E. D. Hirsch Jr., *Cultural Literacy: What Every American Needs to Know* (Boston: Houghton Mifflin, 1987); and Arthur Schlesinger Jr., *The Disuniting of America* (New York: W. W. Norton, 1992).

8. Marvin A. McMickle, "The Black Preacher and Issues of Justice," *African American Pulpit* 2, no. 1 (winter 1998–99): 70–80.

9. Aldon Morris, *The Origins of the Civil Rights Movement* (New York: Free Press, 1984), pp. 4–16.

10. Charles V. Hamilton, *The Black Preacher in America* (New York: Morrow, 1972), pp. 221–22.

11. Daniel E. Payne, *Recollections of Seventy Years* (New York: Arno Press, 1969), p. 153.

12. Benjamin E. Mays, *Born to Rebel* (New York: Scribner's, 1971); and Samuel D. Proctor, *My Moral Odyssey* (Valley Forge, Pa.: Judson Press, 1988).

13. For more about Mary McLeod Bethune, see *African American Voices of Triumph: Leadership* (New York: Time-Life Books, 1994), pp. 222–23.

14. "2 New Hampshire Campuses Address Rise in Racial Tensions," *New York Times*, 1 December 1998, p. A17.

15. Samuel D. Proctor, *The Young Negro in America 1960–1980* (Washington, D.C.: Association Press, 1966).

16. "Three Florida Schools Make List of Top 50 for Black Students," *Cleveland Life*, 16 December 1998, p. 4.

17. "We've Come This Far By Faith," song by Albert A. Goodson. Reprinted in *Songs of Zion* (Nashville: Abingdon Press, 1981), 192.

Chapter 4: Black Middle-Class Churches as Change Agents

1. Earl Shelp and Ronald H. Sunderland, eds. *The Pastor as Servant* (New York: Pilgrim Press, 1986), pp. 63–64.

2. James D. Anderson, *The Education of Blacks in the South, 1860–1935* (Chapel Hill: University of North Carolina Press, 1988).

3. Daniel E. Payne, *Recollections of Seventy Years* (New York: Arno Press, 1969), p. 150.

4. Marvin A. McMickle, *From Pulpit to Politics: Reflections on the Separation of Church and State* (Euclid, Oh.: Williams Custom Publishing, 1998).

5. Ibid., pp. 121–65.

6. Katherine Tate, *From Protest to Politics: The New Black Voters in American Elections* (Cambridge: Harvard University Press, 1993), p. 95.

7. Charles V. Hamilton, *The Black Preacher in America* (New York: Morrow, 1972), pp. 221–22.

8. Robert McAfee Brown, "Confessions of a Political Neophyte," *Christianity and Crisis*, 24 December 1953, p. 186.

9. Carl F. H. Henry, *Christian Countermoves in a Decadent Culture* (Portland: Multnomah, 1986), p. 118.

10. The IRS tax-exempt regulations are discussed in depth by Robert Maddox in *Separation of Church and State: Guarantor of Religious Freedom* (New York: Crossroads Books, 1987), pp. 94, 116.

Chapter 5: Competing for the Loyalty of the Black Middle Class

1. Charles Wesley, *History of Sigma Pi Phi* (New York: Fred Weidner and Son, 1954), p. 26.

2. C. Vann Woodward, *The Strange Career of Jim Crow* (New York: Oxford University Press, 1966), p. 96.

3. Lerone Bennett Jr., *Pioneers in Protest* (Chicago: Johnson Publishing, 1968), pp. 29–42.

4. Harry A. Polski and Ernest Kaiser, *The Negro Almanac* (New York: Bellwether, 1971), p. 925.

5. Ibid., p. 856.

6. Ibid., p. 925.

7. St. Clair Drake and Horace Clayton, *Black Metropolis: A Study of Negro Life in a Northern City* (Chicago: University of Chicago Press, 1945), pp. 658–714.

8. E. Franklin Frazier, *The Black Bourgeoisie* (New York: Collier Books, 1957), p. 162.

9. Ibid., pp. 174–75.

10. Ibid., p. 162.

11. Ibid., p. 126.

12. Cornel West, *Race Matters* (Boston: Beacon Press, 1993), pp. 35–36.

13. D. Mackenzie Brown, *Ultimate Concern: Tillich in Dialogue* (New York: Harper and Row, 1965), pp. 7–9.

14. Lorraine Hansberry, *A Raisin in the Sun* (New York: Signet Books, 1958), p. 61.

15. John Locke, "Second Treatise on Civil Government," in *The Democracy Reader*, ed. Diane Ravitch (New York: HarperCollins, 1992), p. 38.

16. West, *Race Matters*, pp. 35–36.

17. "God of Grace and God of Glory," lyrics by Harry Emerson Fosdick (1930) and music by John Hughes (1907), discussed in Harry Emerson Fosdick, *The Living of These Days* (London: SCM Press, London, 1957), p. 193.

Chapter 6: The Black Middle Class and Responsible Christian Stewardship

1. Benjamin E. Mays, *The Negro's God As Reflected in His Literature* (New York: Atheneum, 1968), pp. 23ff.; James H. Cone, *The Spirituals and the Blues* (New York: Seabury Press, 1972), pp. 14ff.

2. James A. Sanders, *Canon and Community* (Philadelphia: Fortress Press, 1984), p. 56.

3. James A. Sanders, "Hermeneutics," in *The Interpreter's Dictionary of the Bible — Supplementary Volume* (Nashville: Abingdon Press, 1976), p. 406.

4. C. Eric Lincoln and Lawrence H. Mamiya, *The Black Church in the African American Experience* (Durham, N.C.: Duke University Press, 1990), p. 269.

5. Martin Luther King Jr., *Where Do We Go from Here?* (New York: Bantam Books, 1968), p. 156.

Chapter 7: Worship: Bridge or Barrier within the Black Church?

1. W. E. B. Du Bois, *The Souls of Black Folk* (Chicago: A. C. McClurg, 1931), pp. 190–91.

2. Albert Raboteau, *Slave Religion* (New York: Oxford University Press, 1978), pp. 128ff.; cf. Clifton H. Johnson and Paul Radin, *God Struck Me Dead: Religious Conversion Experiences and Autobiographies of Ex-Slaves* (New York: Pilgrim Press, 1969).

3. James Baldwin, *Go Tell It on the Mountain* (New York: Dell, 1953).

4. Wyatt Tee Walker, *The Soul of Black Worship* (New York: Martin Luther King Fellows Press, 1984), p. 2.

5. St. Clair Drake and Horace Clayton, *Black Metropolis: A Study of Negro Life in a Northern City* (Chicago: University of Chicago Press, 1945), p. 670.

6. Henry Mitchell, *Celebration and Experience in Preaching* (Nashville: Abingdon Press, 1990), p. 61.

7. Alan Heimert and Perry Miller, *The Great Awakening* (Indianapolis: Bobbs-Merrill, 1967), pp. 228–30.

8. Ibid., p. 230.

9. Stephen Knoll, sermon delivered at Ashland Theological Seminary, Ashland, Ohio, 29 January 1999.

10. J. Wendell Mapson Jr., *The Ministry of Music in the Black Church* (Valley Forge, Pa.: Judson Press, 1984), p. 22.

11. Mitchell, *Celebration and Experience in Preaching*, p. 26.

12. Melva Costen, "Singing Praise to God," in *African American Religious Studies*, ed. Gayraud S. Wilmore (Durham, N.C.: Duke University Press, 1989), p. 403.

13. Du Bois, *The Souls of Black Folk*, p. 190.

14. Walker, *The Soul of Black Worship*, p. 3.

Chapter 8: To White Churches with Black Middle-Class Members

1. Calvin B. Marshall III, "The Black Church — Its Mission Is Liberation," in *The Black Experience in Religion*, ed. C. Eric Lincoln (Garden City, N.Y.: Doubleday, 1974), p. 162.

2. Lawrence Otis Graham, *Our Kind of People: Inside America's Black Upper Class* (New York: HarperCollins, 1998).

3. Carol V. R. George, *Segregated Sabbaths: Richard Allen and the Rise of Independent Black Churches 1760–1840* (New York: Oxford University Press, 1973).

4. Ibid., p. 55.

5. U.S. Constitution, art. 1, sec. 2, par. 3.

6. Quoted in David M. Reimers, *White Protestantism and the Negro* (New York: Oxford University Press, 1965), p. 186.

7. Martin Luther King Jr., *Why We Can't Wait* (New York: Signet Books, 1964), pp. 89–92.

8. Howard Thurman, *With Head and Heart* (New York: Harcourt Brace Jovanovich, 1979).

9. George, *Segregated Sabbaths*, p. 55.

10. Marshall, "The Black Church," p. 158.

11. George, *Segregated Sabbaths*, p. 63. Jones was ordained a deacon in 1795 and an Episcopal priest in 1804.

12. Ibid., p. 89.

13. Ibid., p. 141.

14. Gayraud S. Wilmore and James H. Cone, *Black Theology: A Documentary History, 1966–1979* (Maryknoll, N.Y.: Orbis Books, 1979), pp. 23–34.

15. Ibid., pp. 268–74.

16. Ibid., pp. 80–89.

17. Ibid., p. 322.

18. Robert T. Newbold, ed., *Black Preaching: Select Sermons in the Presbyterian Tradition* (Philadelphia: Geneva Press, 1977); John M. Burgess, ed., *Black Gospel / White Church* (New York: Seabury Press, 1982); Darryl M. Trimiew, ed., *Out of Mighty Waters: Sermons by African American Disciples of Christ Pastors* (St. Louis: Chalice Press, 1994).

19. Lawrence Lucas, *Black Priest / White Church: Catholics and Racism* (New York: Random House, 1970).

20. James H. Cone, *Black Theology and Black Power* (New York: Seabury Press, 1969), pp. 1–2.

21. Ibid., p. 72.

22. Bill Dedman, "Segregation Persists Despite Fair Housing Act, Chicago Study Finds," *New York Times* @aol.com, 17 February 1999, pp. 1–2.

23. G. Michael Bellinger, "Why I'll Be Marching with Sharpton," *New York Times* @aol.com, 16 February 1999, p. 1.

24. Jeff Sikorovsky, "Crime Is His Color," *Sun Press*, 18 February 1999, p. A1.

25. Andrea Simarkis, "Act of Vandalism Turns Barber's Sign into Racist's Message," *Cleveland Plain Dealer*, 15 February 1999, p. 10B.

26. "Stand Up for Jesus," words by George Duffield, reprinted in *The New National Baptist Hymnal* (Nashville: National Baptist Publishing Board, 1977), p. 394.

Bibliography

Anderson, James D. *The Education of Blacks in the South, 1860–1935*. Chapel Hill: University of North Carolina Press, 1988.

African American Literature. Chicago: Holt, Rinehart and Winston, 1992.

African American Voices of Triumph: Leadership. New York: Time-Life Books, 1994.

Baldwin, James. *Go Tell It on the Mountain*. New York: Dell, 1953.

———. *Notes on a Native Son*. Boston: Beacon Press, 1955.

Bellinger, G. Michael. "Why I'll Be Marching with Sharpton." *New York Times* @aol.com, 16 February 1999.

Bennett, Lerone, Jr. *Pioneers in Protest*. Chicago: Johnson Publishing, 1968.

Brown, D. Mackenzie. *Ultimate Concern: Tillich in Dialogue*. New York: Harper and Row, 1965.

Brown, Robert McAfee. "Confessions of a Political Neophyte." *Christianity and Crisis*, 24 December 1953. p. 186.

Burgess, John M., ed. *Black Gospel/White Church*. New York: Seabury Press, 1982.

Capps, Donald. *Pastoral Counseling and Preaching: A Quest for an Integrated Ministry*. Philadelphia: Westminster Press, 1980.

Clebsch, William, and Charles Jaekle, *Pastoral Care in Historical Perspective*. Englewood Cliffs, N.J.: Prentice Hall, 1964.

Cone, James H. *Black Theology and Black Power*. New York: Seabury Press, 1969.

———. *The Spirituals and the Blues*. New York: Seabury Press, 1972.

Dedman, Bill. "Segregation Persists Despite Fair Housing Act, Chicago Study Finds." *New York Times* @aol.com, 17 February 1999.

Drake, St. Clair, and Horace Clayton. *Black Metropolis: A Study of Negro Life in a Northern City*. Chicago: University of Chicago Press, 1945.

Du Bois, W. E. B. *The Souls of Black Folk*. Chicago: A. C. McClurg, 1931.

Felder, Cain Hope. *Troubling Biblical Waters*. Maryknoll, N.Y.: Orbis Books, 1989.

Fisher, Miles Mark. *Negro Slave Songs in the United States*. New York: Citadel Press, 1953.

Fosdick, Harry Emerson. *The Living of These Days*. London: SCM Press, 1957.

Frazier, E. Franklin. *The Black Bourgeoisie*. New York: Collier Books, 1957.

———. *The Negro in the United States*. New York: Macmillan, 1957.

Gates, Henry Louis, Jr. "Frontline: The Two Nations of Black America." www.pbs.org/wgbh.

Gates, Henry Louis, Jr., and Cornel West. *The Future of the Race*. New York: Vintage, 1996.

George, Carol V. R. *Segregated Sabbaths: Richard Allen and the Rise of Independent Black Churches 1760–1840*. New York: Oxford University Press, 1973.

Graham, Lawrence Otis. *Our Kind of People: Inside America's Black Upper Class*. New York: HarperCollins, 1998.

Hamilton, Charles V. *The Black Preacher in America*. New York: Morrow, 1972.

Hansberry, Lorraine. *A Raisin in the Sun*. New York: Signet Books, 1958.

Harris, Michael W. *The Rise of Gospel Blues*. New York: Oxford University Press, 1992.

Heimert, Alan, and Perry Miller. *The Great Awakening*. Indianapolis: Bobbs-Merrill, 1967.

Henry, Carl F. H. *Christian Countermoves in a Decadent Culture*. Portland: Multnomah, 1986.

Hirsch, E. D., Jr. *Cultural Literacy: What Every American Needs to Know*. Boston: Houghton Mifflin, 1987.

Janofsky, Michael. "After Malaise, a New Mood in Nation's Capitol." *New York Times* @aol.com, 11 November 1998.

Johnson, Clifton H., and Paul Radin. *God Struck Me Dead: Religious Conversion Experiences and Autobiographies of Ex-Slaves*. New York: Pilgrim Press, 1969.

Johnson, Dirk. "Jesse Jackson Jr. Is His Father's Son, but He Reaches beyond the Rainbow." *New York Times*, 3 March 1998.

King, Martin Luther, Jr. *Where Do We Go from Here?* New York: Bantam Books, 1968.

———. *Why We Can't Wait*. New York: Signet Books, 1964.

Kotlowitz, Alex. *There Are No Children Here*. New York: Doubleday, 1991.

Landry, Bart. *The New Black Middle Class*. Berkeley: University of California Press, 1987.

Lewis, John. *Walking with the Wind*. New York: Simon and Schuster, 1998.

Lincoln, C. Eric. "Black Church." *Christianity and Crisis* 30, no. 18 (16 November 1970).

———, ed. *The Black Experience in Religion*. Garden City, N.Y.: Doubleday, 1974.

———. "The Middle Class Mentality." In *Experiences, Struggles, and Hopes in the Black Church*, edited by James S. Gadsen. Nashville: Tidings Press, 1975. pp. 58–68.

Lincoln, C. Eric, and Larry H. Mamiya. *The Black Church in the African American Experience*. Durham, N.C.: Duke University Press, 1990.

Linn, Edmund Holt. *Preaching as Counseling: The Unique Method of Harry Emerson Fosdick*. Valley Forge, Pa.: Judson Press, 1966.

Lucas, Lawrence. *Black Priest/White Church: Catholics and Racism*. New York: Random House, 1970.

Mapson, J. Wendell, Jr. *The Ministry of Music in the Black Church*. Valley Forge, Pa.: Judson Press, 1984.

Mays, Benjamin E. *Born to Rebel*. New York: Scribner's, 1971.

———. *The Negro's God As Reflected in His Literature*. New York: Atheneum, 1968.

McKissick, William. *Beyond Roots: In Search of Blacks in the Bible*. Wenonah, N.J.: Renaissance Productions, 1990.

McMickle, Marvin A. "The Black Preacher and Issues of Justice." *African American Pulpit* 2, no. 1 (winter 1998–99): 70–80.

———. *From Pulpit to Politics: Reflections on the Separation of Church and State*. Euclid, Ohio: Williams Custom Publishing, 1998.

———. "Preaching to the Black Middle Class." *Journal of Preaching* 9, no. 1 (winter 1985). pp. 17–23.

Milbanke, Dana. "Harold Ford Jr. Storms His Father's House." *New York Times Magazine*, 25 October 1998.

Miller, Robert Moats. *Harry Emerson Fosdick: Preacher, Pastor, Prophet*. New York: Oxford University Press, 1985.

Mitchell, Henry. *Celebration and Experience in Preaching*. Nashville: Abingdon Press, 1990.

Morris, Aldon. *The Origins of the Civil Rights Movement*. New York: Free Press, 1984.

Newbold, Robert T., ed. *Black Preaching: Select Sermons in the Presbyterian Tradition*. Philadelphia: Geneva Press, 1977.

Page, Clarence. *Showing My Color: Impolite Essays on Race and Identity*. New York: HarperCollins, 1996.

Paris, Peter. *Black Religious Leaders*. Louisville: Westminster / John Knox Press, 1991.

Payne, Daniel E. *Recollections of Seventy Years*. New York: Arno Press, 1969.

Polski, Harry A., and Ernest Kaiser. *The Negro Almanac*. New York: Bellwether, 1971.

Proctor, Samuel D. *My Moral Odyssey*. Valley Forge, Pa.: Judson Press, 1988.

———. *The Young Negro in America 1960–1980*. Washington, D.C.: Association Press, 1966.

Raboteau, Albert. *Slave Religion*. New York: Oxford University Press, 1978.

Ravitch, Diane, ed. *The Democracy Reader*. New York: HarperCollins, 1992.

Reimers, David M. *White Protestantism and the Negro*. New York: Oxford University Press, 1965.

Report of the National Advisory Commission on Civil Disorders. New York: Bantam Books, 1968.

Roberts, J. Deotis. *Roots of a Black Future: Family and Church*. Philadelphia: Westminster Press, 1980.

Robinson, Randall. *Defending the Spirit: A Black Life in America*. New York: Plume Books, 1998.

Rymer, Russ. "Integration's Casualties." *New York Times Magazine*, 1 November 1998.

Sanders, James A. *Canon and Community*. Philadelphia: Fortress Press, 1984.

———. "Hermeneutics." In *The Interpreter's Dictionary of the Bible — Supplemental Volume*. Nashville: Abingdon Press, 1976.

Schlesinger, Arthur, Jr. *The Disuniting of America*. New York: W. W. Norton, 1992.

Shelp, Earl, and Ronald H. Sunderland, eds. *The Pastor as Servant*. New York: Pilgrim Press, 1986.

Sikorovsky, Jeff. "Crime Is His Color." *Sun Press*, 18 February 1999.

Simarkis, Andrea. "Act of Vandalism Turns Barber's Sign into Racist's Message." *Cleveland Plain Dealer*, 15 February 1999.

Sitkoff, Harvard. *The Struggle for Black Equality*. New York: HarperCollins, 1981.

Tate, Katherine. *From Protest to Politics: The New Black Voters in American Elections*. Cambridge: Harvard University Press, 1993.

"Three Florida Schools Make List of Top 50 for Black Students." *Cleveland Life*, 16 December 1998.

Thurman, Howard. *With Head and Heart*. New York: Harcourt Brace Jovanovich, 1979.

Trimiew, Darryl M., ed. *Out of Mighty Waters: Sermons by African American Disciples of Christ Pastors*. St. Louis: Chalice Press, 1994.

"2 New Hampshire Campuses Address Rise in Racial Tensions." *New York Times*, 1 December 1998.

Walker, Wyatt Tee. *Somebody's Calling My Name*. Valley Forge, Pa.: Judson Press, 1979.

———. *The Soul of Black Worship*. New York: Martin Luther King Fellows Press, 1984.

Wesley, Charles. *History of Sigma Pi Phi*. New York: Fred Weidner and Son, 1954.

West, Cornel. *Race Matters*. Boston: Beacon Press, 1993.

Wilmore, Gayraud S. *African American Religious Studies*. Durham, N.C.: Duke University Press, 1989.

Wilmore, Gayraud S., and James H. Cone, eds. *Black Theology: A Documentary History, 1966–1979*. Maryknoll, N.Y.: Orbis Books, 1979.

Wilson, William Julius. *The Declining Significance of Race*. Chicago: University of Chicago Press, 1988.

Wimberly, Edward P. *Pastoral Care in the Black Church*. Nashville: Abingdon Press, 1979.

Woodward, C. Vann. *The Strange Career of Jim Crow*. New York: Oxford University Press, 1966.